John M. Synge

Riders to the Sea
and
The Playboy of
the Western World

with Introduction and Notes by
E. R. WOOD

HEINEMANN EDUCATIONAL BOOKS · LONDON

Heinemann Educational Books Ltd

LONDON EDINBURGH MELBOURNE TORONTO
SINGAPORE JOHANNESBURG AUCKLAND IBADAN
HONG KONG NAIROBI NEW DELHI
KUALA LUMPUR

ISBN 0 435 22868 4

RIDERS TO THE SEA
First published 1905

THE PLAYBOY OF THE WESTERN WORLD
First published 1907

This edition first published 1961
Reprinted 1962, 1963, 1966, 1967, 1971, 1972

Published by
Heinemann Educational Books Ltd
48 Charles Street, London W1X 8AH
Printed Offset Litho and Bound in Great Britain by
Cox & Wyman Ltd., London, Fakenham and Reading

Contents

RIDERS TO THE SEA was first performed on 25 February 1904 in the Molesworth Hall, Dublin, with the following cast:

MAURYA	Honor Lavelle
BARTLEY	W. G. Fay
CATHLEEN	Sara Allgood
NORA	Emma Vernon

THE PLAYBOY OF THE WESTERN WORLD was first performed on 26 January 1907, at the Abbey Theatre, Dublin with the following cast:

CHRISTOPHER MAHON	W. G. Fay
OLD MAHON	A. Power
MICHAEL JAMES FLAHERTY	Arthur Sinclair
MARGARET FLAHERTY (Pegeen Mike)	Maire O'Neill
SHAWN KEOGH	F. J. Fay
PHILLY O'CULLEN	J. A. O'Rourke
JIMMY FARRELL	J. M. Kerrigan
WIDOW QUIN	Sara Allgood
SARA TANSEY	Brigit O'Dempsey
SUSAN BRADY	Alice O'Sullivan
HONOR BLAKE	May Craig
PEASANTS	U. Wright, Harry Young

THE PLAYBOY OF THE WESTERN WORLD has been recorded on two 33 r.p.m. discs, Columbia CCX 4 and 5, with Cyril Cusack as Christy and Siobhan McKenna as Pegeen.

163705

QUEEN MARGARET COLLEGE

LIBRARY

Please return book on or before latest date
stamped below

INTRODUCTION
by E. R. Wood

J. M. SYNGE AND THE IRISH THEATRE

Some of the greatest playwrights of the English theatre – Goldsmith, Sheridan, Shaw, Wilde – were Irishmen, but they did not write primarily about Ireland or for the Irish; they came to England both for inspiration and for recognition.

At the end of the last century Yeats and others set out to create (or revive) a native Irish culture. They were convinced that Irish folk tales and myths recalling the past glories of Ireland could bring fresh life and vigour to literature. Such a renaissance, together with the revival of the Irish language (then almost extinct) would help to stimulate the Irish nationalism which sought to throw off the English political yoke and cultural dominance. Moreover, Yeats thought (rightly) that the Irish had something of their own to contribute to European culture. He was particularly contemptuous of English middle-class values.

The Irish Literary Theatre was formed in 1899. At first English actors performed in Dublin new plays by Irishmen such as Yeats and George Moore. The movement might soon have died but for the emergence of two gifted Irish amateur actors, the brothers William and Frank Fay, round whom was built the Irish National Dramatic Company. This company needed new plays by Irish writers, and it found many; its greatest 'find' was Synge.

John M. Synge (pronounced *Sing*) was born in Dublin in 1871 and educated at Trinity College. Afterwards he wandered through France, Germany and Italy, devoting himself to music and literature. Yeats found him living in a poor quarter of Paris, and persuaded him that he needed to go back to Ireland for inspiration. He stayed for long periods in the Aran Islands off the western coast and lived elsewhere as a peasant among peasants, absorbing their stories, their attitude to life and their colourful language. These are the people whom we see in his plays.

The first fruit of Synge's stay in the remote West of Ireland was *The Shadow of the Glen*. This was one of the plays which the Irish Players brought to London in 1903, when they enjoyed a sensational triumph. One eminent critic wrote: 'The players were like a summer breeze to jaded London,' and A. B. Walkley in *The Times* said: 'A little band of Irish men and women, strangers to London and Londoners, gave some of us who, for our sins, are constant frequenters of the playhouse, a few moments of calm delight quite outside the range of anything which these houses have to offer.' A practical result of their success was an offer by an enthusiastic member of the audience to provide the money necessary to establish in Dublin a permanent Irish theatre. The benefactor was Miss A. E. F. Horniman, a wealthy patron of the drama (she also promoted famous repertory theatres in Manchester and Liverpool), who gave £13,000 to found the Abbey Theatre.

When the company revisited London in April, 1904, the packed audience included leaders of the political and literary worlds as well as dramatic critics of the first rank. Max Beerbohm called the occasion 'one of the rare oases in the desert of our drama'. C. E. Montague was enthusiastic about both the acting and the plays, especially *Riders to the Sea*. 'The play in a few moments thrills whole theatres to the kind of hush that comes when Othello approaches the sleeping Desdemona,' he wrote later*. 'Synge, from the first, is as terse, as exacting, as strange as he likes; yet everyone sees what he means, and all of his people have the tragic importance. ... No such gift has been made to modern Ireland by any of her children as Synge's disengagement of the essence, the differentiating virtue of the native imagination in Irish country folk.'

* in Dramatic Values.

THE PLAYBOY OF THE WESTERN WORLD

STORMY RECEPTION

While the plays of Synge brought honour to the Abbey Theatre throughout the English-speaking world, the Dublin audiences received them with noisy hostility. *The Playboy of The Western World* provoked particularly angry scenes. For a whole week the performances were violently interrupted. Some shouted and hissed; some blew trumpets; some threw missiles. It was clear that the actors were confronted with an organised attempt to suppress the play. The actors doggedly went through it in dumb show; police were called in to try to keep order; the management refused to be daunted. Disturbances have been almost a tradition of the Abbey Theatre, reaching their most dangerous pitch in the riots provoked some twenty years later by Sean O'Casey's *The Plough and the Stars*. Noisy controversy in the theatre is no doubt healthier than well-bred apathy, and it is understandable that before the Irish achieved their independence some of them were readily resentful of anything that seemed to belittle Irish life and character. All the same, it is difficult today to see what all the fuss over *The Playboy* was about.

Some people thought that Synge, a Protestant, was discrediting the Catholic Irish, but if there is any satire on simple people's religious beliefs and practices, it is such as many a good Catholic might himself indulge in. More obtuse was the solemn objection that Irish people do not behave like the characters in the play, condoning murder and encouraging lies. The character of Pegeen was considered to be an insult to Irish womanhood; even the Fay brothers begged Synge to make Pegeen a 'decent, likeable country girl' and to remove the offensive scene where the villagers scorch Christy's leg. Some of Synge's friends and admirers thought there was too much bad language, and audiences found certain lines shocking. One line in particular, about 'a drift of chosen females standing in their shifts' evoked outraged protests. Yeats was not present at the first performance but he received two telegrams reporting the reception of the play. The first, sent off after the first act, said 'Play great success'. The second said: 'Audience broke up in disorder at the word *shift*'.

Yeats returned to Dublin and led the stubborn struggle to keep the play going in defiance of the opposition, and in the end he won. But the hostility was not merely the product of narrow-minded and provincial Dubliners; the reception of the play was stormy in the United States wherever Irish nationalists were in the audience.

THEMES OF *The Playboy*

After allowances have been made for the patriotic Irishmen who resented *The Playboy* as an attack on their countrymen, it does seem nevertheless that they were a little humourless and cantankerous. The play is a gay comedy in which the Mayo villagers are laughable but likeable. Synge was no more anti-Irish than Molière was anti-French or Shakespeare anti-English; indeed, he was himself a profound admirer of the Irish peasants, though he did not sentimentalise them.

The admiration of the Mayo peasants for a fugitive from justice is understandable in a simple people accustomed to think of the law as alien – as indeed it was, insofar as it was English law imposed on a defiant nation. 'The impulse to protect the criminal,' wrote Synge in *The Aran Islands*, 'is universal in the West. It seems partly due to the association between justice and the hated English jurisdiction, but more directly to the primitive feeling of these people, who are never criminals yet always capable of crime, that a man will not do wrong unless he is under the influence of a passion which is as irresponsible as the sea.' This is why they welcome 'fine, fiery fellows with great rages when their temper's roused.' The events of the play are based on an actual case of a man who had killed his father being hidden by Aran Islanders until he was able to escape to America.

But it is misleading to consider this as a problem play about parricide. After all, Christy did not kill his father and the peasants did not approve when he tried. The important thing about them is that they love a bold story of a daring fellow. Christy's standing rises as his tale grows taller; they all help to build it up, until he can declare: 'From this out I'll have no want of company when all sorts is bringing me their food and clothing, the way they'd set their eyes on a gallant orphan cleft his father with one blow to the breeches belt'. His father too has benefited from the widespread love of a strange tale. 'I'm after walking hundreds and long scores of miles,' he says, 'winning clean beds and the fill of my belly four times in the day, and I doing nothing but telling stories of that naked truth'. At the end, as he and Christy are about to turn their backs on the village, he looks forward to 'great times ... telling stories of the villainy of Mayo and the fools is here'. This engaging fondness for a brave story is connected with a sense of wonder at the 'big world' beyond the limited horizon of their ordinary life. They have heard of such marvels as the rows of ancient skulls in a Dublin museum; they think of a stranger 'living like a king of Norway or the Eastern World'; and they talk grandly of 'great powers and potentates of France and Spain'. The traveller from this outside world brings with him some gleams of its splendour, stirring their imaginations and enriching their lives. This need for a heroic vision beyond the trivial round is one of the serious themes in this boisterous comedy.

The play also expresses a modest psychological truth contained in an old Irish saying: 'Praise Youth and it will prosper'. While everyone treated Christy as a stupid lout he *was* a stupid lout. When he comes among people who treat him as a romantic hero, he becomes a hero. He develops powers hitherto unknown to himself; he wins the racing and the lepping; his eloquence stirs the heart of Pegeen and his masterful spirit dominates the village. When the bubble bursts with the reappearance of Old Mahon, and Christy attempts to do what they thought he had done, he finds it is not the deed that they had all admired, but the splendid tale. 'A strange man is a marvel with his mighty talk,' says Pegeen, 'but there's a great gap between a gallous story and a dirty deed.' The villagers have awakened from the heroic dream to find the actuality ugly and squalid.

But for Christy, the dream has come true. His newly-discovered powers are real, and he is not now to be daunted. These people have made of him a fine, stout lad, and they cannot destroy what they have made. This is why the end of the play is a triumph for Christy. 'Ten thousand blessings upon all that's here,' he says, 'for you've turned me into a likely gaffer in the end of all, the way I'll go romancing through a romping lifetime from this hour to the dawning of the Judgment Day'. His father, who now has a son to be proud of, says, 'Glory be to God!', and it is Pegeen who laments, 'I've lost the only Playboy of the Western World.'

A more conventional playwright would have ended with Christy and Pegeen reconciled and about to marry. Synge's is a 'happy ending' for Christy, but of an astringent, unsentimental kind. It is more important for the new Christy that he can now stand up to his father than that he should win the girl who has fallen short of his romantic picture of her. She had seemed 'an angel's lamp' to him: when she encourages his tormentors he sees her without illusions. 'That's your kind, is it?' he says: and now he is free of her. This makes it clear that the conclusion is concerned with Christy's emancipation, not Pegeen's heart.

It has been suggested that Christy's revolt against his father is symbolical of Ireland's wish to throw off English Rule. As Christy finally realises his dream of what he could be, so, according to this reading, might Ireland look forward to a nobler future. Interesting as this theory may be to think out, there seems to be no evidence that Synge himself was aware of it.

DRAMATIC QUALITIES OF *The Playboy*

The Playboy of the Western World has, then, something serious to say about people in communities, but it is above all a lively comedy. The playwright seeks to extract from his characters and his themes primarily those ingredients that create theatrical excitement and fun. Synge was misunderstood not only by those who disliked what they thought he was saying, but also by admirers who wanted the play taken more seriously. A. E. Malone, a distinguished historian of the Abbey Theatre, complained in his book *The Irish Drama* (1929) that the great actor Arthur Sinclair had been guilty of playing for laughs in serious plays. 'The audience could be induced to laugh uproariously at Sinclair even in such plays as *The Shadow of the Glen* and *The Playboy of the Western World*' (Sinclair played Michael James, the publican). In the face of such criticism it is perhaps necessary to repeat that *The Playboy* is a boisterous comedy.

Part of the fun is in the sheer paradox of a youth basking in admiration because he has committed a hideous crime (or says he has). Such a paradox is exploited and underlined when the conventional forms of piety mingle in the story: when Pegeen asks Christy if he killed his father he replies, 'With the help of God I did, surely' and Jimmy comments, 'Oh, glory be to God!' To object that father-killing is wicked and godless is to miss the joke of the paradox. A delightful development of the paradox is in Christy's reply when Pegeen asks if he *shot* his father. 'I never used weapons,' he says. 'I've no licence, and I'm a law-fearing man.'

The development of Christy's story is the stuff of essential comedy (compare Falstaff's story of the fight at Gadshill), rising to a delightful peak when he demonstrates with a chicken bone the details of how he split his father to the knob of his gullet. It reaches its comic climax when Christy, swaggering about how he cleft his father with one blow to the breeches belt, opens the door, to find to his horror that his father is coming. Indeed, there are times when the playwright's craft appears perhaps a little too obviously: Old Mahon keeps coming in at the most theatrical moment: Jimmy has just said; 'A man can't hang by his own informing, and his father should be rotten by now', when Old Mahon passes the window. Later Michael has just said: 'A daring fellow is the jewel of the world, and a man did split his father's middle with a single clout should have the bravery of ten, so may God and Mary and St Patrick bless you and increase you from this mortal day', when Old Mahon rushes in and knocks Christy down. At such times the more sophisticated playgoer, finding the theatrical tricks a little too mechanical, is reminded of a line in *King Lear:* 'And pat he comes, like the vice in the old comedy.'

The theatrical appearances of Old Mahon are examples of a pervading feature of comedy: ironic contrast. This is very effectively exploited throughout the play. There is throughout the first act the contrast between Christy on his arrival, 'a slight, young man, very tired and frightened and dirty', and the 'fine handsome fellow with a noble brow' that Pegeen sees in him as soon as she hears that he is a fugitive from the law. As is mentioned above, the gap between the two Christies is comically stressed when Old Mahon arrives. It is further exploited in the scene that follows, where Old Mahon describes to the Widow Quin the 'small, low fellow, dark and dirty' who was 'the laughing joke of every female woman where four baronies meet.'

There is further contrast between the expanding Christy with his mighty spirit and exuberant eloquence on the one hand, and the wretched abject Shawn on the other, 'a middling scarecrow with no savagery or fine words in him at all.' Contrast of tone is theatrically effective when a beautiful love-duet between Pegeen and Christy, leading to the conclusion, 'Well, the heart's a wonder; and I'm thinking, there won't be our like in Mayo for gallant lovers from this hour today', is interrupted by drunken singing heralding the arrival of Michael James from the boisterous celebration of a funeral.

The play is very clearly constructed. Each act falls into a series of short scenes, each having its own climax and often contrasted in tone with an adjacent one, as in the example just mentioned. Some critics have suggested that in the dramatic structure the opening of the second act is a weakness. Throughout the first act we have been aware of the spiritual presence of Old Mahon and, according to Frank O'Connor[1], 'from the rise of the curtain on the second, we should be made ready for his entrance, should see that bandaged, raging man crawling up through Ireland, drawing ever nearer – perhaps it is he, surely it is; here he comes.' Hence the scenes with the village girls, in this view, are an irrelevance. On the other hand, they serve the necessary purpose of showing Christy developing in the sunshine of female admiration from 'the looney of Mahon's' into one of the 'wonders of the Western World.' He has his setbacks, too, and gains the opportunity to see Pegeen in a harsher light. This helps him (and the audience) at the end.

THE LANGUAGE

The quality of the dialogue is obviously an essential feature of any play. In the Preface to *The Playboy* Synge says: 'In a good

1 In *The Irish Theatre*, ed. Lennox Robinson (Macmillan 1939).

play every speech should be as fully flavoured as a nut or apple' and he acknowledges that Irish playwrights have great advantages in that Irish people still speak a rich and vigorous English. In *The Playboy* even more than in other plays of Synge the splendour of the language is of the essence of the theme, since the villagers have a highly developed taste for 'mighty talk' and Christy's eloquence is the most impressive of his gifts. He is capable of such poetic flights as when he speaks of 'squeezing kisses on your puckered lips, till I'd feel a kind of pity for the Lord God is all ages sitting lonesome in His golden chair' or 'If the mitred bishops seen you that time, they'd be like the holy prophets, I'm thinking, do be straining the bars of Paradise to lay eyes on the Lady Helen of Troy, and she abroad, pacing back and forwards, with a nosegay in her golden shawl.' Even when the realistic Widow Quin seeks to bring him down to earth by scoffing at his poetry talk about 'a girl you'd see itching and scratching and she with a stale stink of poteen on her from selling in the shop', he replies, 'It's her like is fitted to be handling merchandise in the heavens above.' In the dialogue that follows, Christy's images are all of the heavens, while the Widow's mind is on mundane realities.

> CHRISTY: Aid me for to win her, and I'll be asking God to stretch a hand to you in the hour of death, and lead you short cuts through the Meadows of Ease, and up the floor of Heaven to the Footstool of the Virgin's Son.
> WIDOW QUIN: If I aid you, will you swear to give me a right of way I want, and a mountainy ram, and a load of dung at Michaelmas, the time you'll be master here?
> CHRISTY: I will, by the elements and stars of night.

The load of dung is effectively set in contrast with the floor of Heaven.

But it is not only his love of Pegeen that inspires Christy's eloquence. The less poetic subject of his drunken father evokes a picture full of vivid life: 'He after drinking for weeks, rising up in the red dawn, or before it maybe, and going out into the yard as naked as an ash tree in the moon of May, and shying clods against the visage of the stars...' What splendid extravagance! As if 'naked as an ash tree' were not colourful simile enough, he must add 'in the moon of May'. The disreputable old drunkard shies clods not merely at the sky but at 'the visage of the stars'. Christy cares not only for a clear picture, but also for a fine rolling phrase. He is a master of hyperbole: threatening his tormentors, he promises 'a blow unto the lot of you would set the guardian angels winking in the clouds above'. When he expresses his horror that Pegeen is ready to hand him over to justice, he visualises with harsh realism, every word adding a brutal detail, 'a horny-fingered hangman hitching his bloody slip-knots at the butt of my ear'.

Of course, Christy is not alone in his eloquence. Pegeen catches some of its tone, though she has a strong practical side that brings her poetic flights down to a narrower scale as in: 'If that's the truth, I'll be burning candles from this out to the miracles of God that have brought you from the south today, and I with my gowns ready, the way that I can wed you, and not wait at all.' The same mixture of the poetic and the earthy is used for comic effect in her father, in whose mouth reverence for the dead and for holiness jostles with a pagan relish for drink at funerals: 'Arn't you a louty schemer to go burying your father unbeknownst when you'd a right to throw him on the crupper of a Kerry mule and drive him westwards, like holy Joseph in the days gone by, the way we could have given him a decent burial, and not have him rotting beyond, and not a Christian drinking a smart drop to the glory of his soul?' or 'When we sunk her bones at noonday in her narrow grave, there were five men, aye and six men, stretched out retching speechless on the holy stones.' As in Christy, there is also a lively appetite for the ring of words.

Synge claimed in the Preface that he had heard on the lips of

Irish people almost every word or phrase used in the play. This is not to say that the Irish anywhere speak quite so well as his characters. Synge accentuated the vigour, the poetic fancy, the rhythmical quality, the sonority and the quaintness of Anglo-Irish idiom to produce a heightened language that can sound like natural speech and at the same time stir the imagination and delight the ear like poetry. It is, in fact, what Wordworth called 'a selection of the real language of men in a state of vivid sensation'.

It is worth analysing some of the features of this Anglo-Irish poetry-prose. There are very many turns of phrase and quaint constructions that originally came into Anglo-Irish speech from the Gaelic. Very common is the participal or other phrase joined to the main clause by the conjunction *and*, as in 'My heart's scalded this day, and I going off stretching the earth between us' or 'You'd be making him a son to me, and he wet and crusted with his father's blood?' Then, instead of a perfect tense, we find the present tense with *after*; for example, instead of 'You have won', 'You're after winning all in the sports below'. Very frequently the verb *to be* is used to throw emphasis on a particular word or phrase that follows it: 'It's on my naked knees I'd be saying my prayers and paters' or 'Is it me fight him, when it's father-slaying he's bred to now?' In ordinary English, such emphasis would more often be conveyed by the tone of voice. The emphatic personal pronoun is commoner than in English, as in 'Where's himself?' or 'Where is he itself?' The relative pronoun if oftener omitted than in England, as in 'It was the divil's own mirorr we had beyond, (that) would twist a squint across an angel's brow'. A direct imperative is formed with the auxiliary *let*: 'Let you wait' or 'Let you take it'. Such accumulated quaintnesses of phrase, typical of ordinary Irish dialect, do not necessarily make the dialogue more poetic or more expressive; but they do help to provide an escape from the flat, conventional language of much middle-class English chatter.

When we listen to the rhythm of Synge's dialogue we are aware of recurring cadences that are not those of ordinary prose, nor even of the beautiful literary prose which Synge himself wrote in such works as *The Aran Islands*. Common phrases like 'at the fall of dark', 'in the heat of noon', 'when the night is down', all contain the same stress-pattern (u u / u /) which recurs surprisingly often at the ends of sentences. Longer recurring stress-patterns can be traced as in

'Wild and windy acres of rich Munster land',
'You'll be strangling one another in a score of days',
'I'll make myself contented to be lodging here'.

Often the rhythmical pattern is accentuated by alliteration, as in 'powers and potentates', 'walking the world', 'toiling, moiling, digging, dodging from dawn till dusk', or 'a prison behind him, and hanging before, and hell's gap gaping below'.

Sometimes Synge's rhythms make for monotony and the critical reader may feel that the playwright is too consciously manipulating sounds and syllables to please the ear. On the whole, however, the effect is a remarkably successful blend of naturalism and poetry. Rhythmically, this language is different from that of other major Irish dramatists such as Sean O'Casey and Denis Johnston. For a more startling contrast, it is interesting to look at any page of such modern English plays as *Roots*, *A Taste of Honey* or *The Birthday Party*.

But it is not so much in the Gaelic constructions or in the rhythmical patterns that the real richness of Synge's dialogue is achieved, as in the expressive words and similes. It is for these that Synge acknowledges his debt to the Irish peasants to whom he has listened. Here are no 'joyless and pallid words'. Whether his characters are expressing extravagant splendour ('the young gaffer who'd capsize the stars') or rude abuse ('a hideous, fearful villain, and the spit of you') they never want for words. The similes (always fire-new) are not for decoration, but to make a picture alive: 'I'll flatten you out like a crawling beast has passed under a dray', 'Your whole skin needing washing like a Wicklow sheep'; 'He'd be off to hide in the sticks, and you'd see him shooting out his sheep's eyes between the twigs and leaves, and his two ears rising like a hare looking out through a gap'. All these similes belong to the familiar peasant world. Christy, for all his magniloquence in which his similes soar to the heavens of Christian and pagan gods, can describe a sordid existence in sentences where every word adds to the definition of the picture: 'We were digging spuds in his cold, sloping, stony, divil's patch of a field.' The language is always appropriate to the character and to the mood or time of the scene.

RIDERS TO THE SEA

THEMES OF THE PLAY

Riders to the Sea shows us similar people (but more specifically the Aran Islanders) in a totally different light. *The Playboy* is concerned with problems of how human beings should behave towards each other: *Riders to the Sea* shows how men should conduct themselves in the face of Fate. If the essence of drama is Conflict, then the principal character is the sea, the instrument of Fate. These Aran Islanders know that men who ride to the sea must expect hardship and early death, and they meet both with stoical resignation.

In *The Aran Islands* Synge expressed profound admiration for these primitive people, who, he said, 'seem to approach more nearly to the finer types of our aristocracies than to the labourer or the citizen, as the wild horse resembles the thoroughbred rather than the hack or carthorse'. So the characters in the play, though preoccupied with the day-to-day problems of their humble struggle for subsistence – whether they have enough turf for the fire, whether the sheep will jump in on the rye, or whether there is enough bread for the men making the coffin – have a noble awareness of the importance of life and the need to show proper respect for the dignity of death.

The play has often been compared to a Greek tragedy because of the view of life and death here implied. 'Call no man happy until he is dead', said Solon, and similar words conclude the *Oedipus* of Sophocles. In Greek Tragedy man does not expect happiness in life, though he hopes to live it nobly, meet his end stoically and be honoured in death.

Maurya is comforted by the thought that one of her sons has had a clean burial in the far North and another will have a deep grave. 'What more can we want than that?' she asks. 'No man at all can be living for ever, and we must be satisfied.'

So, although these are humble people compared with the exalted heroes of Greek Tragedy, they are similar in their austere conception of life and death. Life has to be lived as a struggle, but it must have dignity. The play is full of realistic detail such as the dropped stitch that identifies the stocking and so proves that Michael is dead, or the water dripping on the dry stones as the drowned Bartley is carried in. At the same time the ceremonial customs such as giving a blessing before a journey, or keening and praying over a corpse, are a recognition of mysterious forces beyond the scope of daily life. Death is elemental. Faced with the problems of everyday life, we are individual men and women: faced with Death, we are part of Mankind.

DRAMATIC QUALITIES OF THE PLAY

Riders to the Sea also resembles Greek Tragedy in the austere conception of what makes a play. The plot is utterly bare and simple. Most of the actual events happen (or have happened) off-stage, and the dramatic experience is not in the exciting clash of physical action. It is rather in the awareness of a pattern of events being worked out according to the demands of Fate.

Nevertheless, things do happen, and in a clear dramatic structure. This falls into a series of short scenes or movements, each having its own action and its distinct tone, the whole rising from Exposition to a Climax, followed by the calm of Anti-climax. In the opening exposition we learn something of what has happened and is to happen. The tone is quietly realistic. The preoccupations of Norah and Cathleen are personal and immediate: they must examine the clothes found on a drowned man to see if they belonged to their brother Michael, and they must do so without the knowledge of their mother, Maurya. The next movement is a conflict of wills in which Maurya fails to dissuade Bartley from going away by the next boat. This is also realistic and stark. Bartley's mind is so full of such immediate details as making a halter for the horse, selling the pig with black feet, or getting in more seaweed from the shore, that he hardly replies to his mother. At the same time we are aware, through Maurya, of profounder values beside which the selling of the horse is unimportant. When Bartley has gone, the very credible incident of the forgotten bread serves first to get rid of Maurya while the girls examine the clothes and confirm that the drowned man was Michael (this movement has a clear climax) and then to bring her back, still holding the bread, with the terribly prophetic story of her vision. Here the tone changes, since Maurya is no longer merely a particular old woman: she is essential Woman, prophetically aware of the dark mysteries of life and death. Synge then exploits the situation to produce a highly theatrical moment, the climax of the play: Maurya is describing how, many years ago, the body of one of her sons was carried in, when the door opens and her story is re-enacted with the body of the drowned Bartley. We learn how events have borne out Maurya's prophetic vision. The conclusion is concerned with eternals: Maurya's Lament is for her family and for all riders to the sea. In the calm of all passion spent, she is reconciled to God's will.

THE LANGUAGE

The dialogue has many of the characteristics of Anglo-Irish speech noticed in *The Playboy*, but the general effect is very different, as should be expected. The lively exuberance of the

comic dialogue would be inappropriate here, and the extravagant splendour of Christy's eloquence would serve no purpose.
The most obvious difference is the absence of simile. The
language is spare, stripped of decoration.

As in *The Playboy*, the speech is more rhythmical than
normal, but its rhythms are different, less buoyant, The tragic
mood is expressed in falling cadences at the ends of sentences, as
in 'It's getting old she is, and broken,' or 'No man at all can
be living for ever, and we must be satisfied.

There is often a formality near to poetry or music, especially
in the longer speeches of Maurya. Here (and elsewhere) it is
worth noting the effect of repetition:

'I'll have no call now to be up crying and praying when the
wind breaks from the south, and you can hear the surf is in the
east, and the surf is in the west . . . I'll have no call now to be
going down and getting Holy Water . . . It isn't that I haven't
prayed for you, Bartley, to the Almighty God. It isn't that I
haven't said prayers in the dark night . . .'

Most of the gusto and colour of *The Playboy* have been
sacrificed to the austere mood; there remains much that is
vivid, moving and beautiful.

RIDERS TO THE SEA

PERSONS IN THE PLAY

MAURYA, *an old Woman*
BARTLEY, *her Son*
CATHLEEN, *her Daughter*
NORA, *a younger Daughter*
MEN AND WOMEN

SCENE – *An Island off the West of Ireland*

RIDERS TO THE SEA

*Cottage kitchen, with nets, oilskins, spinning-wheel, some new
boards standing by the wall, etc.* CATHLEEN, *a girl of about
twenty, finishes kneading cake, and puts it down in the pot-oven
by the fire; then wipes her hands, and begins to spin at the wheel.*
NORA, *a young girl, puts her head in at the door.*

NORA (*in a low voice*): Where is she?

CATHLEEN: She's lying down, God help her, and maybe
sleeping, if she's able.

    NORA *comes in softly, and takes a bundle from under her shawl.*

CATHLEEN (*spinning the wheel rapidly*): What is it you have?

NORA: The young priest is after bringing them. It's a shirt and
a plain stocking were got off a drowned man in Donegal.

    CATHLEEN *stops her wheel with a sudden movement, and leans
out to listen.*

NORA: We're to find out if it's Michael's they are, some time
herself will be down looking by the sea.

CATHLEEN: How would they be Michael's, Nora? How would
he go the length of that way to the far north?

NORA: The young priest says he's known the like of it. 'If it's
Michael's they are,' says he, 'you can tell herself he's got a
clean burial, by the grace of God; and if they're not his, let no
one say a word about them, for she'll be getting her death,'
says he, 'with crying and lamenting.'

    The door which NORA *half closed is blown open by a gust of
wind.*

CATHLEEN (*looking out anxiously*): Did you ask him would he
stop Bartley going this day with the horses to the Galway
fair?

NORA: 'I won't stop him,' says he; 'but let you not be afraid.

Herself does be saying prayers half through the night, and the Almighty God won't leave her destitute,' says he, 'with no son living.'

CATHLEEN: Is the sea bad by the white rocks, Nora?

NORA: Middling bad, God help us. There's a great roaring in the west, and it's worse it'll be getting when the tide's turned to the wind. (*She goes over to the table with the bundle*) Shall I open it now?

CATHLEEN: Maybe she'd wake up on us, and come in before we'd done (*coming to the table*). It's a long time we'll be, and the two of us crying.

NORA (*goes to the inner door and listens*): She's moving about on the bed. She'll be coming in a minute.

CATHLEEN: Give me the ladder, and I'll put them up in the turf-loft, the way she won't know of them at all, and maybe when the tide turns she'll be going down to see would he be floating from the east.

They put the ladder against the gable of the chimney; CATHLEEN *goes up a few steps and hides the bundle in the turf-loft.* MAURYA *comes from the inner room.*

MAURYA (*looking up at* CATHLEEN *and speaking querulously*): Isn't it turf enough you have for this day and evening?

CATHLEEN: There's a cake baking at the fire for a short space (*throwing down the turf*), and Bartley will want it when the tide turns if he goes to Connemara.

NORA picks up the turf and puts it round the pot-oven.

MAURYA (*sitting down on a stool at the fire*): He won't go this day with the wind rising from the south and west. He won't go this day, for the young priest will stop him surely.

NORA: He'll not stop him, mother; and I heard Eamon Simon and Stephen Pheety and Colum Shawn saying he would go.

MAURYA: Where is he itself?

NORA: He went down to see would there be another boat sailing in the week, and I'm thinking it won't be long till he's here now, for the tide's turning at the green head, and the hooker's tacking from the east.

CATHLEEN: I hear some one passing the big stones.

NORA (*looking out*): He's coming now, and he in a hurry.

BARTLEY (*comes in and looks round the room. Speaking sadly and quietly*): Where is the bit of new rope, Cathleen, was bought in Connemara?

CATHLEEN (*coming down*): Give it to him, Nora; it's on a nail by the white boards. I hung it up this morning, for the pig with the black feet was eating it.

NORA (*giving him a rope*): Is that it, Bartley?

MAURYA: You'd do right to leave that rope, Bartley, hanging by the boards (BARTLEY *takes the rope*). It will be wanting in this place, I'm telling you, if Michael is washed up to-morrow morning, or the next morning; or any morning in the week; for it's a deep grave we'll make him, by the grace of God.

BARTLEY (*beginning to work with the rope*): I've no halter the way I can ride down on the mare, and I must go now quickly. This is the one boat going for two weeks or beyond it, and the fair will be a good fair for horses, I heard them saying below.

MAURYA: It's a hard thing they'll be saying below if the body is washed up and there's no man in it to make the coffin, and I after giving a big price for the finest white boards you'd find in Connemara.

She looks round at the boards.

BARTLEY: How would it be washed up, and we after looking each day for nine days, and a strong wind blowing a while back from the west and south?

MAURYA: If it isn't found itself, that wind is raising the sea, and there was a star up against the moon, and it rising in the night. If it was a hundred horses, or a thousand horses, you had itself, what is the price of a thousand horses against a son where there is one son only?

BARTLEY (*working at the halter, to* CATHLEEN): Let you go down each day, and see the sheep aren't jumping in on the rye, and if the jobber comes you can sell the pig with the black feet if there is a good price going.

MAURYA: How would the like of her get a good price for a pig?

BARTLEY (*to* CATHLEEN): If the west wind holds with the last bit of the moon let you and Nora get up weed enough for another cock for the kelp. It's hard set we'll be from this day with no one in it but one man to work.

MAURYA: It's hard set we'll be surely the day you're drowned with the rest. What way will I live and the girls with me, and I an old woman looking for the grave?

BARTLEY *lays down the halter, takes off his old coat, and puts on a newer one of the same flannel.*

BARTLEY (*to* NORA): Is she coming to the pier?

NORA (*looking out*): She's passing the green head and letting fall her sails.

BARTLEY (*getting his purse and tobacco*): I'll have half an hour to go down, and you'll see me coming again in two days, or in three days, or maybe in four days if the wind is bad.

MAURYA (*turning round to the fire, and putting her shawl over her head*): Isn't it a hard and cruel man won't hear a word from an old woman, and she holding him from the sea?

CATHLEEN: It's the life of a young man to be going on the sea, and who would listen to an old woman with one thing and she saying it over?

BARTLEY (*taking the halter*): I must go now quickly. I'll ride down on the red mare, and the grey pony'll run behind me. . . . The blessing of God on you.

He goes out.

MAURYA (*crying out as he is in the door*): He's gone now, God spare us, and we'll not see him again. He's gone now, and when the black night is falling I'll have no son left me in the world.

CATHLEEN: Why wouldn't you give him your blessing and he looking round in the door? Isn't it sorrow enough is on every one in this house without your sending him out with an unlucky word behind him, and a hard word in his ear?

MAURYA takes up the tongs and begins raking the fire aimlessly without looking round.

NORA (*turning towards her*): You're taking away the turf from the cake.

CATHLEEN (*crying out*): The Son of God forgive us, Nora, we're after forgetting his bit of bread.

She comes over to the fire.

NORA: And it's destroyed he'll be going till dark night, and he after eating nothing since the sun went up.

CATHLEEN (*turning the cake out of the oven*): It's destroyed he'll be, surely. There's no sense left on any person in a house where an old woman will be talking for ever.

MAURYA sways herself on her stool.

CATHLEEN (*cutting off some of the bread and rolling it in a cloth; to MAURYA*): Let you go down now to the spring well and give him this and he passing. You'll see him then and the dark word will be broken, and you can say 'God speed you,' the way he'll be easy in his mind.

MAURYA (*taking the bread*): Will I be in it as soon as himself?

CATHLEEN: If you go now quickly.

MAURYA (*standing up unsteadily*): It's hard set I am to walk.

CATHLEEN (*looking at her anxiously*): Give her the stick, Nora, or maybe she'll slip on the big stones.

NORA: What stick?

CATHLEEN: The stick Michael brought from Connemara.

MAURYA (*taking a stick NORA gives her*): In the big world the old people do be leaving things after them for their sons and children, but in this place it is the young men do be leaving things behind for them that do be old.

She goes out slowly. NORA goes over to the ladder.

CATHLEEN: Wait, Nora, maybe she'd turn back quickly. She's that sorry, God help her, you wouldn't know the thing she'd do.

NORA: Is she gone round by the bush?

CATHLEEN (*looking out*): She's gone now. Throw it down quickly, for the Lord knows when she'll be out of it again.

NORA (*getting the bundle from the loft*): The young priest said he'd be passing to-morrow, and we might go down and speak to him below if it's Michael's they are surely.

CATHLEEN (*taking the bundle*): Did he say what way they were found?

NORA (*coming down*): 'There were two men,' says he, 'and they rowing round with poteen before the cocks crowed, and the oar of one of them caught the body, and they passing the black cliffs of the north.'

CATHLEEN (*trying to open the bundle*): Give me a knife, Nora; the string's perished with the salt water, and there's a black knot on it you wouldn't loosen in a week.

NORA (*giving her a knife*): I've heard tell it was a long way to Donegal.

CATHLEEN (*cutting the string*): It is surely. There was a man here a while ago – the man sold us that knife – and he said if you set off walking from the rocks beyond, it would be in seven days you'd be in Donegal.

NORA: And what time would a man take, and he floating?

CATHLEEN *opens the bundle and takes out a bit of shirt and a stocking. They look at them eagerly.*

CATHLEEN (*in a low voice*): The Lord spare us, Nora! Isn't it a queer hard thing to say if it's his they are surely?

NORA: I'll get his shirt off the hook the way we can put the one flannel on the other. (*She looks through some clothes hanging in the corner*). It's not with them, Cathleen, and where will it be?

CATHLEEN: I'm thinking Bartley put it on him in the morning, for his own shirt was heavy with the salt in it. (*Pointing to the corner.*) There's a bit of a sleeve was of the same stuff. Give me that and it will do.

NORA *brings it to her and they compare the flannel.*

CATHLEEN: It's the same stuff, Nora; but if it is itself, aren't there great rolls of it in the shops of Galway, and isn't it many another man may have a shirt of it as well as Michael himself?

NORA (*who has taken up the stocking and counted the stitches, crying out*): It's Michael, Cathleen, it's Michael; God spare his soul, and what will herself say when she hears this story, and Bartley on the sea?

CATHLEEN (*taking the stocking*): It's a plain stocking.

NORA: It's the second of the third pair I knitted, and I put up three-score stitches, and I dropped four of them.

CATHLEEN (*counts the stitches*): It's that number is in it. (*Crying out*) Ah, Nora, isn't it a bitter thing to think of him floating that way to the far north, and no one to keen him but the black hags that do be flying on the sea?

NORA (*swinging herself half-round, and throwing out her arms on the clothes*): And isn't it a pitiful thing when there is nothing left of a man who was a great rower and fisher but a bit of an old shirt and a plain stocking?

CATHLEEN (*after an instant*): Tell me is herself coming, Nora? I hear a little sound on the path.

NORA (*looking out*): She is, Cathleen. She's coming up to the door.

CATHLEEN: Put these things away before she'll come in. Maybe it's easier she'll be after giving her blessing to Bartley, and we won't let on we've heard anything the time he's on the sea.

NORA (*helping* CATHLEEN *to close the bundle*): We'll put them here in the corner.

They put them into a hole in the chimney corner. CATHLEEN *goes back to the spinning-wheel.*

NORA: Will she see it was crying I was?

CATHLEEN: Keep your back to the door the way the light'll not be on you.

NORA sits down at the chimney corner, with her back to the door.

c

MAURYA *comes in very slowly, without looking at the girls, and goes over to her stool at the other side of the fire. The cloth with the bread is still in her hand. The girls look at each other, and* NORA *points to the bundle of bread.*

CATHLEEN (*after spinning for a moment*): You didn't give him his bit of bread?

MAURYA *begins to keen softly, without turning round.*

CATHLEEN: Did you see him riding down?

MAURYA *goes on keening.*

CATHLEEN (*a little impatiently*): God forgive you; isn't it a better thing to raise your voice and tell what you seen, than to be making lamentation for a thing that's done? Did you see Bartley, I'm saying to you?

MAURYA (*with a weak voice*): My heart's broken from this day.

CATHLEEN (*as before*): Did you see Bartley?

MAURYA: I seen the fearfulest thing.

CATHLEEN (*leaves her wheel and looks out*): God forgive you; he's riding the mare now over the green head, and the grey pony behind him.

MAURYA (*starts, so that her shawl falls back from her head and shows her white tossed hair. With a frightened voice*): The grey pony behind him. . . .

CATHLEEN (*coming to the fire*): What is it ails you at all?

MAURYA (*speaking very slowly*): I've seen the fearfullest thing any person has seen since the day Bride Dara seen the dead man with the child in his arms.

CATHLEEN AND NORA: Uah.

They crouch down in front of the old woman at the fire.

NORA: Tell us what it is you seen.

MAURYA: I went down to the spring well, and I stood there saying a prayer to myself. Then Bartley came along, and he riding on the red mare with the grey pony behind him (*She puts up her hands, as if to hide something from her eyes.*) The Son of God spare us, Nora!

CATHLEEN: What is it you seen?

MAURYA: I seen Michael himself.

CATHLEEN (*speaking softly*): You did not, mother. It wasn't Michael you seen, for his body is after being found in the far north, and he's got a clean burial, by the grace of God.

MAURYA (*a little defiantly*): I'm after seeing him this day, and he riding and galloping. Bartley came first on the red mare, and I tried to say 'God speed you,' but something choked the words in my throat. He went by quickly: and 'the blessing of God on you,' says he, and I could say nothing. I looked up then, and I crying, at the grey pony, and there was Michael upon it – with fine clothes on him, and new shoes on his feet.

CATHLEEN (*begins to keen*): It's destroyed we are from this day. It's destroyed surely.

NORA: Didn't the young priest say the Almighty God won't leave her destitute with no son living?

MAURYA (*in a low voice, but clearly*): It's little the like of him knows of the sea. . . . Bartley will be lost now, and let you call in Eamon and make me a good coffin out of the white boards, for I won't live after them. I've had a husband, and a husband's father, and six sons in this house – six fine men, though it was a hard birth I had with every one of them and they coming to the world – and some of them were found and some of them were not found, but they're gone now the lot of them. . . . There were Stephen and Shawn were lost in the great wind, and found after in the Bay of Gregory of the Golden Mouth, and carried up the two of them on one plank, and in by that door.

She pauses for a moment, the girls start as if they heard something through the door that is half open behind them.

NORA (*in a whisper*): Did you hear that, Cathleen? Did you hear a noise in the north-east?

CATHLEEN (*in a whisper*): There's some one after crying out by the seashore.

MAURYA (*continues without hearing anything*): There was Sheamus and his father, and his own father again, were lost in a dark night, and not a stick or sign was seen of them when the sun went up. There was Patch after was drowned out of a curagh that turned over. I was sitting here with Bartley, and he a baby lying on my two knees, and I seen two women and three women, and four women coming in, and they crossing themselves and not saying a word. I looked out then, and there were men coming after them, and they holding a thing in the half of a red sail, and water dripping out of it – it was a dry day, Nora – and leaving a track to the door.

She pauses again with her hand stretched out towards the door. It opens softly and OLD WOMEN *begin to come in, crossing themselves on the threshold, and kneeling down in front of the stage with red petticoats over their heads.*

MAURYA (*half in a dream, to* CATHLEEN): Is it Patch, or Michael, or what is it at all?

CATHLEEN: Michael is after being found in the far north, and when he is found there how could he be here in this place?

MAURYA: There does be a power of young men floating round in the sea, and what way would they know if it was Michael they had, or another man like him, for when a man is nine days in the sea, and the wind blowing, it's hard set his own mother would be to say what man was in it.

CATHLEEN: It's Michael, God spare him, for they're after sending us a bit of his clothes from the far north.

She reaches out and hands MAURYA *the clothes that belonged to Michael.* MAURYA *stands up slowly, and takes them in her hands.* NORA *looks out.*

NORA: They're carrying a thing among them, and there's water dripping out of it and leaving a track by the big stones.

CATHLEEN (*in a whisper to the women who have come in*): Is it Bartley it is?

ONE OF THE WOMEN: It is, surely, God rest his soul.

TWO YOUNGER WOMEN come in and pull out the table. Then men carry in the body of Bartley, laid on a plank, with a bit of sail over it, and lay it on the table.

CATHLEEN (*to the women as they are doing so*): What way was he drowned?

ONE OF THE WOMEN: The grey pony knocked him over into the sea, and he was washed out where there is a great surf on the white rocks.

MAURYA *has gone over and knelt down at the head of the table.* THE WOMEN *are keening softly and swaying themselves with a slow movement.* CATHLEEN *and* NORA *kneel at the other end of the table.* THE MEN *kneel near the door.*

MAURYA (*raising her head and speaking as if she did not see the people around her*): They're all gone now, and there isn't anything more the sea can do to me.... I'll have no call now to be up crying and praying when the wind breaks from the south, and you can hear the surf is in the east, and the surf is in the west, making a great stir with the two noises, and they hitting one on the other. I'll have no call now to be going down and getting Holy Water in the dark nights after Samhain, and I won't care what way the sea is when the other women will be keening. (*To* NORA.) Give me the Holy Water, Nora; there's a small sup still on the dresser.

NORA *gives it to her.*

MAURYA (*drops Michael's clothes across* BARTLEY'S *feet, and sprinkles the Holy Water over him*): It isn't that I haven't prayed for you, Bartley, to the Almighty God. It isn't that I haven't said prayers in the dark night till you wouldn't know what I'd be saying; but it's a great rest I'll have now, and it's time, surely. It's a great rest I'll have now, and great sleeping in the long nights after Samhain, if it's only a bit of wet flour we do have to eat, and maybe a fish that would be stinking.

She kneels down again, crossing herself, and saying prayers under her breath.

CATHLEEN (*to an old man*): Maybe yourself and Eamon would make a coffin when the sun rises. We have fine white boards herself bought, God help her, thinking Michael would be found, and I have a new cake you can eat while you'll be working.

THE OLD MAN (*looking at the boards*): Are there nails with them?

CATHLEEN: There are not, Colum; we didn't think of the nails.

ANOTHER MAN: It's a wonder she wouldn't think of the nails, and all the coffins she's seen made already.

CATHLEEN: It's getting old she is, and broken.

MAURYA stands up again very slowly and spreads out the pieces of Michael's clothes beside the body, sprinkling them with the last of the Holy Water.

NORA (*in a whisper to* CATHLEEN): She's quiet now and easy; but the day Michael was drowned you could hear her crying out from this to the spring well. It's fonder she was of Michael, and would anyone have thought that?

CATHLEEN (*slowly and clearly*): An old woman will be soon tired with anything she will do, and isn't it nine days herself is after crying and keening, and making great sorrow in the house?

MAURYA (*puts the empty cup mouth downwards on the table, and lays her hands together on* BARTLEY's *feet*): They're all together this time, and the end is come. May the Almighty God have mercy on Bartley's soul, and on Michael's soul, and on the souls of Sheamus and Patch, and Stephen and Shawn (*bending her head*); and may He have mercy on my soul, Nora, and on the soul of everyone is left living in the world.

She pauses, and the keen rises a little more loudly from the women, then sinks away.

MAURYA (*continuing*): Michael has a clean burial in the far north, by the grace of the Almighty God. Bartley will have a fine coffin out of the white boards, and a deep grave surely. What more can we want than that? No man at all can be living for ever, and we must be satisfied.

She kneels down again and the curtain falls slowly.

THE PLAYBOY OF THE WESTERN WORLD

PERSONS IN THE PLAY

CHRISTOPHER MAHON
OLD MAHON, *his father, a squatter*
MICHAEL JAMES FLAHERTY (called MICHAEL JAMES), *a publican*
MARGARET FLAHERTY (called PEGEEN MIKE), *his daughter*
SHAWN KEOGH, *her cousin, a young farmer*
WIDOW QUIN, *a woman of about thirty*
PHILLY CULLEN and JIMMY FARREL, *small farmers*
SARA TANSEY, SUSAN BRADY, NELLY and HONOR BLAKE, *village girls*
A BELLMAN
SOME PEASANTS

The action takes place near a village, on a wild coast of Mayo. The first Act passes on an evening of autumn, the other two Acts on the following day.

PREFACE

In writing THE PLAYBOY OF THE WESTERN WORLD, as in my other plays, I have used one or two words only that I have not heard among the country people of Ireland, or spoken in my own nursery before I could read the newspapers. A certain number of the phrases I employ I have heard also from herds and fishermen along the coast from Kerry to Mayo, or from beggar-women and ballad-singers nearer Dublin; and I am glad to acknowledge how much I owe to the folk-imagination of these fine people. Anyone who has lived in real intimacy with the Irish peasantry will know that the wildest sayings and ideas in this play are tame indeed, compared with the fancies one may hear in any little hillside cabin in Geesala, or Carraroe, or Dingle Bay. All art is a collaboration; and there is little doubt that in the happy ages of literature, striking and beautiful phrases were as ready to the story-teller's or the playwright's hand, as the rich cloaks and dresses of his time. It is probable that when the Elizabethan dramatist took his ink-horn and sat down to his work he used many phrases that he had just heard, as he sat at dinner, from his mother or his children. In Ireland, those of us who know the people have the same privilege. When I was writing *The Shadow of the Glen*, some years ago, I got more aid than any learning could have given me from a chink in the floor of the old Wicklow house where I was staying, that let me hear what was being said by the servant girls in the kitchen. This matter, I think, is of importance, for in countries where the imagination of the people, and the language they use, is rich and living, it is possible for a writer to be rich and copious in his words, and at the same time to give the reality, which is the root of all poetry, in a comprehensive and natural form. In the modern literature of towns, however, richness is found only in sonnets, or prose poems, or in one or two elaborate books that are far away from the profound and common interests of life. One has, on one side, Mallarmé and Huysmans producing this literature; and on the other, Ibsen and Zola dealing with the reality of life in joyless and pallid words. On the stage one must have reality, one must have joy; and that is why the intellectual modern drama has failed, and people have grown sick of the false joy of the musical comedy, that has been given them in place of the rich joy found only in what is superb and wild in reality. In a good play every speech should be as fully flavoured as a nut or apple, and such speeches cannot be written by anyone who works among people who have shut their lips on poetry. In Ireland, for a few years more, we have a popular imagination that is fiery, and magnificent and tender; so that those of us who wish to write start with a chance that is not given to writers in places where the spring-time of the local life has been forgotten, and the harvest is a memory only, and the straw has been turned into bricks.

J. M. S.

January 21, 1907.

ACT ONE

*Country public-house or shebeen, very rough and untidy. There is a
sort of counter on the right with shelves, holding many bottles and
jugs, just seen above it. Empty barrels stand near the counter. At
back, a little to left of counter, there is a door into the open air, then,
more to the left, there is a settle with shelves above it, with more
jugs, and a table beneath a window. At the left there is a large
open fire-place, with turf fire, and a small door into inner room.*
PEEGEN, *a wild-looking but fine girl, of about twenty, is writing
at table. She is dressed in the usual peasant dress.*

PEGEEN (*slowly as she writes*): Six yards of stuff for to make a
  yellow gown. A pair of lace boots with lengthy heels on
  them and brassy eyes. A hat is suited for a wedding-day. A
  fine-tooth comb. To be sent with three barrels of porter in
  Jimmy Farrell's creel cart on the evening of the coming Fair
  to Mister Michael James Flaherty. With the best compliments
  of this season. Margaret Flaherty.

SHAWN KEOGH (*a fat and fair young man, comes in as she signs,
  looks round awkwardly, when he sees she is alone*): Where's
  himself?

PEGEEN (*without looking at him*): He's coming. (*She directs
  letter.*) To Mister Sheamus Mulroy, Wine and Spirit Dealer,
  Castlebar.

SHAWN (*uneasily*): I didn't see him on the road.

PEGEEN: How would you see him (*licks stamp and puts it on
  letter*) and it dark night this half hour gone by?

SHAWN (*turning towards door again*): I stood a while outside
  wondering would I have a right to pass on or to walk in and

see you, Pegeen Mike (*comes to fire*), and I could hear the cows breathing and sighing in the stillness of the air, and not a step moving any place from this gate to the bridge.

PEGEEN (*putting letter in envelope*): It's above at the cross-roads he is, meeting Philly Cullen and a couple more are going along with him to Kate Cassidy's wake.

SHAWN (*looking at her blankly*): And he's going that length in dark night.

PEGEEN (*impatiently*): He is surely, and leaving me lonesome on the scruff of the hill. (*She gets up and puts envelope on dresser, then winds the clock.*) Isn't it long the nights are now, Shawn Keogh, to be leaving a poor girl with her own self counting the hours to the dawn of day?

SHAWN (*with awkward humour*): If it is, when we're wedded in a short while you'll have no call to complain, for I've little will to be walking off to wakes or weddings in the darkness of the night.

PEGEEN (*with rather scornful good-humour*): You're making mighty certain, Shaneen, that I'll wed you now.

SHAWN: Aren't we after making a good bargain, the way we're only waiting these days on Father Reilly's dispensation from the bishops, or the Court of Rome.

PEGEEN (*looking at him teasingly, washing up at dresser*): It's a wonder, Shaneen, the Holy Father'd be taking notice of the likes of you; for if I was him I wouldn't bother with this place where you'll meet none but Red Linahan, has a squint in his eye, and Patcheen is lame in his heel or the mad Mulrannies were driven from California and they lost in their wits. We're a queer lot these times to go troubling the Holy Father on his sacred seat.

SHAWN (*scandalized*): If we are, we're as good this place as another, maybe, and as good these times as we were for ever.

PEGEEN (*with scorn*): As good, is it? Where now will you meet the like of Danny Sullivan knocked the eye from a peeler; or

Marcus Quin, God rest him, got six months for maiming ewes and he a great warrant to tell stories of holy Ireland till he'd have the old women shedding down tears about their feet. Where will you find the like of them, I'm saying?

SHAWN (*timidly*): If you don't, it's a good job, maybe; for (*with peculiar emphasis on the words*) Father Reilly has small conceit to have that kind walking around and talking to the girls.

PEGEEN (*impatiently, throwing water from basin out of the door*): Stop tormenting me with Father Reilly (*imitating his voice*) when I'm asking only what way I'll pass these twelve hours of dark, and not take my death with the fear. (*Looking out of door.*)

SHAWN (*timidly*): Would I fetch you the Widow Quin, maybe?

PEGEEN: Is it the like of that murderer? You'll not, surely.

SHAWN (*going to her, soothingly*): Then I'm thinking himself will stop along with you when he sees you taking on; for it'll be a long night-time with great darkness, and I'm after feeling a kind of fellow above in the furzy ditch, groaning wicked like a maddening dog, the way it's good cause you have, maybe, to be fearing now.

PEGEEN (*turning on him sharply*): What's that? Is it a man you seen?

SHAWN (*retreating*): I couldn't see him at all; but I heard him groaning out, and breaking his heart. It should have been a young man from his words speaking.

PEGEEN (*going after him*): And you never went near to see was he hurted or what ailed him at all?

SHAWN: I did not, Pegeen Mike. It was a dark, lonesome place to be hearing the like of him.

PEGEEN: Well, you're a daring fellow, and if they find his corpse stretched above in the dews of dawn, what'll you say then to the peelers, or the Justice of the Peace?

SHAWN (*thunderstruck*): I wasn't thinking of that. For the love of God, Pegeen Mike, don't let on I was speaking of him. Don't tell your father and the men is coming above; for if they heard that story, they'd have great blabbing this nigh at the wake.

PEGEEN: I'll maybe tell them, and I'll maybe not.

SHAWN: They are coming at the door. Will you whisht, I'm saying?

PEGEEN: Whisht yourself.

She goes behind counter. MICHAEL JAMES, *fat, jovial publican, comes in followed by* PHILLY CULLEN, *who is thin and mistrusting, and* JIMMY FARRELL, *who is fat and amorous, about forty-five.*

MEN (*together*): God bless you! The blessing of God on this place!

PEGEEN: God bless you kindly.

MICHAEL (*to men, who go to the counter*): Sit down now, and take your rest. (*Crosses to* SHAWN *at the fire.*) And how is it you are, Shawn Keogh? Are you coming over the sands to Kate Cassidy's wake?

SHAWN: I am not, Michael James. I'm going home the short cut to my bed.

PEGEEN (*speaking across the counter*): He's right, too, and have you no shame, Michael James, to be quitting off for the whole night, and leaving myself lonesome in the shop?

MICHAEL (*good-humouredly*): Isn't it the same whether I go for the whole night or a part only? and I'm thinking it's a queer daughter you are if you'd have me crossing backward through the Stooks of the Dead Women, with a drop taken.

PEGEEN: If I am a queer daughter, it's a queer father'd be leaving me lonesome these twelve hours of dark, and I piling the turf with the dogs barking, and the calves mooing, and my own teeth rattling with the fear.

JIMMY (*flatteringly*): What is there to hurt you, and you a fine, hardy girl would knock the head of any two men in the place?

PEGEEN (*working herself up*): Isn't there the harvest boys with their tongues red for drink, and the ten tinkers is camped in

the east glen, and the thousand militia – bad cess to them! –
walking idle through the land. There's lots surely to hurt me,
and I won't stop alone in it, let himself do what he will.

MICHAEL: If you're that afeard, let Shawn Keogh stop along
with you. It's the will of God, I'm thinking, himself should
be seeing to you now.

They all turn on SHAWN.

SHAWN (*in horrified confusion*): I would and welcome, Michael
James, but I'm afeard of Father Reilly; and what at all would
the Holy Father and the Cardinals of Rome be saying if they
heard I did the like of that?

MICHAEL (*with contempt*): God help you! Can't you sit in by
the hearth with the light lit and herself beyond in the room?
You'll do that surely, for I've heard tell there's a queer fellow
above, going mad or getting his death, maybe, in the gripe
of the ditch, so she'd be safer this night with a person here.

SHAWN (*with plaintive despair*): I'm afeard of Father Reilly, I'm
saying. Let you not be tempting me, and we near married
itself.

PHILLY (*with cold contempt*): Lock him in the west room. He'll
stay then and have no sin to be telling to the priest.

MICHAEL (*to SHAWN, getting between him and the door*): Go up
now.

SHAWN (*at the top of his voice*): Don't stop me, Michael James.
Let me out of the door, I'm saying, for the love of the Almighty God. Let me out (*trying to dodge past him*). Let me out
of it, and may God grant you His indulgence in the hour of
need.

MICHAEL (*loudly*): Stop your noising, and sit down by the
hearth.

Gives him a push and goes to counter laughing.

SHAWN (*turning back, wringing his hands*): Oh, Father Reilly and
the saints of God, where will I hide myself to-day? Oh, St
Joseph and St Patrick and St Brigid and St James, have
mercy on me now!

SHAWN *turns round, sees door clear, and makes a rush for it.*

MICHAEL (*catching him by the coat-tail*): You'd be going, is it?

SHAWN (*screaming*): Leave me go, Michael James, leave me go, you old Pagan, leave me go, or I'll get the curse of the priests on you, and of the scarlet-coated bishops of the Courts of Rome.

With a sudden movement he pulls himself out of his coat, and disappears out of the door, leaving his coat in MICHAEL'S *hands.*

MICHAEL (*turning round, and holding up coat*): Well, there's the coat of a Christian man. Oh, there's sainted glory this day in the lonesome west; and by the will of God I've got you a decent man, Pegeen, you'll have no call to be spying after if you've a score of young girls, maybe, weeding in your fields.

PEGEEN (*taking up the defence of her property*): What right have you to be making game of a poor fellow for minding the priest, when it's your own the fault is, not paying a penny pot-boy to stand along with me and give me courage in the doing of my work?

She snaps the coat away from him, and goes behind counter with it.

MICHAEL (*taken aback*): Where would I get a pot-boy? Would you have me send the bell-man screaming in the streets of Castlebar?

SHAWN (*opening the door a chink and putting in his head, in a small voice*): Michael James!

MICHAEL (*imitating him*): What ails you?

SHAWN: The queer dying fellow's beyond looking over the ditch. He's come up, I'm thinking, stealing your hens. (*Looks over his shoulder.*) God help me, he's following me now (*he runs into room*), and if he's heard what I said, he'll be having my life, and I going home lonesome in the darkness of the night.

For a perceptible moment they watch the door with curiosity. Someone coughs outside. Then CHRISTY MAHON, *a slight young man, comes in very tired and frightened and dirty.*

CHRISTY (*in a small voice*): God save all here!

MEN: God save you kindly!

CHRISTY (*going to the counter*): I'd trouble you for a glass of porter, woman of the house. (*He puts down coin.*)

PEGEEN (*serving him*): You're one of the tinkers, young fellow, is beyond camped in the glen?

CHRISTY: I am not; but I'm destroyed walking.

MICHAEL (*patronizingly*): Let you come up then to the fire. You're looking famished with the cold.

CHRISTY: God reward you! (*He takes up his glass and goes a little way across to the left, then stops and looks about him.*) Is it often the polis do be coming into this place, master of the house?

MICHAEL: If you'd come in better hours, you'd have seen 'Licensed for the Sale of Beer and Spirits, to be Consumed on the Premises,' written in white letters above the door, and what would the polis want spying on me, and not a decent house within four miles, the way every living Christian is a bona fide, saving one widow alone?

CHRISTY (*with relief*): It's a safe house, so.

He goes over to the fire, sighing and moaning. Then he sits down, putting his glass beside him, and begins gnawing a turnip, too miserable to feel the others staring at him with curiosity.

MICHAEL (*going after him*): Is it yourself is fearing the polis? You're wanting, maybe?

CHRISTY: There's many wanting.

MICHAEL: Many, surely, with the broken harvest and the ended wars. (*He picks up some stockings, etc., that are near the fire, and carries them away furtively.*) It should be larceny, I'm thinking?

CHRISTY (*dolefully*): I had it in my mind it was a different word and a bigger.

PEGEEN: There's a queer lad. Were you never slapped in school, young fellow, that you don't know the name of your deed?

D

CHRISTY (*bashfully*): I'm slow at learning, a middling scholar only.

MICHAEL: If you're a dunce itself, you'd have a right to know that larceny's robbing and stealing. Is it for the like of that you're wanting?

CHRISTY (*with a flash of family pride*): And I the son of a strong farmer (*with a sudden qualm*), God rest his soul, could have bought up the whole of your old house a while since, from the butt of his tail-pocket, and not have missed the weight of it gone.

MICHAEL (*impressed*): If it's not stealing, it's maybe something big.

CHRISTY (*flattered*): Aye; it's maybe something big.

JIMMY: He's a wicked-looking young fellow. Maybe he followed after a young woman on a lonesome night.

CHRISTY (*shocked*): Oh, the saints forbid, mister; I was all times a decent lad.

PHILLY (*turning on* JIMMY): You're a silly man, Jimmy Farrell. He said his father was a farmer a while since, and there's himself now in a poor state. Maybe the land was grabbed from him, and he did what any decent man would do.

MICHAEL (*to* CHRISTY, *mysteriously*): Was it bailiffs?

CHRISTY: The divil a one.

MICHAEL: Agents?

CHRISTY: The divil a one.

MICHAEL: Landlords?

CHRISTY (*peevishly*): Ah, not at all, I'm saying. You'd see the like of them stories on any little paper of a Munster town. But I'm not calling to mind any person, gentle, simple, judge or jury, did the like of me.

They all draw nearer with delighted curiosity.

PHILLY: Well, that lad's a puzzle-the-world.

JIMMY: He'd beat Dan Davies' circus, or the holy missioners making sermons on the villainy of man. Try him again, Philly.

PHILLY: Did you strike golden guineas out of solder, young fellow, or shilling coins itself?

CHRISTY: I did not, mister, not sixpence nor a farthing coin.

JIMMY: Did you marry three wives maybe? I'm told there's a sprinkling have done that among the holy Luthers of the preaching north.

CHRISTY (*shyly*): I never married with one, let alone with a couple or three.

PHILLY: Maybe he went fighting for the Boers, the like of the man beyond, was judged to be hanged, quartered, and drawn. Were you off east, young fellow, fighting bloody wars for Kruger and the freedom of the Boers?

CHRISTY: I never left my own parish till Tuesday was a week.

PEGEEN (*coming from counter*): He's done nothing, so. (*To* CHRISTY.) If you didn't commit murder or a bad, nasty thing; or false coining, or robbery, or butchery, or the like of them, there isn't anything that would be worth your troubling for to run from now. You did nothing at all.

CHRISTY (*his feelings hurt*): That's an unkindly thing to be saying to a poor orphaned traveller, has a prison behind him, and hanging before, and hell's gap gaping below.

PEGEEN (*with a sign to the men to be quiet*): You're only saying it. You did nothing at all. A soft lad the like of you wouldn't slit the wind-pipe of a screeching sow.

CHRISTY (*offended*): You're not speaking the truth.

PEGEEN (*in mock rage*): Not speaking the truth, is it? Would you have me knock the head of you with the butt of the broom?

CHRISTY (*twisting round on her with a sharp cry of horror*): Don't strike me. I killed my poor father, Tuesday was a week, for doing the like of that.

PEGEEN (*with blank amazement*): Is it killed your father?

CHRISTY (*whistling*): With the help of God I did, surely, and that the Holy Immaculate Mother may intercede for his soul.

PHILLY (*retreating with* JIMMY): There's a daring fellow.

JIMMY: Oh, glory be to God!

MICHAEL (*with great respect*): That was a hanging crime, mister honey. You should have had good reason for doing the like of that.

CHRISTY (*in a very reasonable tone*): He was a dirty man, God forgive him, and he getting old and crusty, the way I couldn't put up with him at all.

PEGEEN: And you shot him dead?

CHRISTY (*shaking his head*): I never used weapons. I've no licence, and I'm a law-fearing man.

MICHAEL: It was with a hilted knife maybe? I'm told, in the big world, it's bloody knives they use.

CHRISTY (*loudly, scandalized*): Do you take me for a slaughter-boy?

PEGEEN: You never hanged him, the way Jimmy Farrell hanged his dog from the licence, and had it screeching and wriggling three hours at the butt of a string, and himself swearing it was a dead dog, and the peelers swearing it had life?

CHRISTY: I did not, then. I just riz the loy and let fall the edge of it on the ridge of his skull, and he went down at my feet like an empty sack, and never let a grunt or groan from him at all.

MICHAEL (*making a sign to* PEGEEN *to fill* CHRISTY's *glass*): And what way weren't you hanged, mister? Did you bury him then?

CHRISTY (*considering*): Aye. I buried him then. Wasn't I digging spuds in the field?

MICHAEL: And the peelers never followed after you the eleven days that you're out?

CHRISTY (*shaking his head*): Never a one of them, and I walking forward facing hog, dog, or divil on the highway of the road.

PHILLY (*nodding wisely*): It's only with a common week-day

kind of a murderer them lads would be trusting their
carcase, and that man should be a great terror when his
temper's roused.

MICHAEL: He should then. (*To* CHRISTY.) And where was it,
mister honey, that you did the deed?

CHRISTY (*looking at him with suspicion*): Oh, a distant place,
master of the house, a windy corner of high, distant hills.

PHILLY (*nodding with approval*): He's a close man, and he's
right, surely.

PEGEEN: That's be a lad with the sense of Solomon to have for
a pot-boy, Michael James, if it's truth you're seeking one at
all.

PHILLY: The peelers is fearing him, and if you'd that lad in the
house there isn't one of them would come smelling around
if the dogs itself were lapping poteen from the dung-pit of
the yard.

JIMMY: Bravery's a treasure in a lonesome place, and a lad
would kill his father, I'm thinking, would face a foxy divil
with a pitchpike on the flags of hell.

PEGEEN: It's the truth they're saying, and if I'd that lad in the
house, I wouldn't be fearing the loosèd kharki cut-throats, or
the walking dead.

CHRISTY (*swelling with surprise and triumph*): Well, glory be to
God!

MICHAEL (*with deference*): Would you think well to stop here
and be pot-boy, mister honey, if we gave you good wages,
and didn't destroy you with the weight of work?

SHAWN (*coming forward uneasily*): That'd be a queer kind to
bring into a decent, quiet household with the like of Pegeen
Mike.

PEGEEN (*very sharply*): Will you whisht? Who's speaking to
you?

SHAWN (*retreating*): A bloody-handed murderer the like of . . .

PEGEEN (*snapping at him*): Whisht, I am saying; we'll take no
fooling from your like at all. (*To* CHRISTY *with a honeyed*

voice.) And you, young fellow, you'd have a right to stop, I'm thinking, for we'd do our all and utmost to content your needs.

CHRISTY (*overcome with wonder*): And I'd be safe this place from the searching law?

MICHAEL: You would, surely. If they're not fearing you, itself, the peelers in this place is decent, drouthy, poor fellows, wouldn't touch a cur dog and not giving warning in the dead of night.

PEGEEN (*very kindly and persuasively*): Let you stop a short while anyhow. Aren't you destroyed walking with your feet in bleeding blisters, and your whole skin needing washing like a Wicklow sheep.

CHRISTY (*looking round with satisfaction*): It's a nice room, and if it's not humbugging me you are, I'm thinking that I'll surely stay.

JIMMY (*jumps up*): Now, by the grace of God, herself will be safe this night, with a man killed his father holding danger from the door, and let you come on, Michael James, or they'll have the best stuff drunk at the wake.

MICHAEL (*going to the door with men*): And begging your pardon, mister, what name will we call you, for we'd like to know?

CHRISTY: Christopher Mahon.

MICHAEL: Well, God bless you, Christy, and a good rest till we meet again when the sun'll be rising to the noon of day.

CHRISTY: God bless you all.

MEN: God bless you.

They go out, except SHAWN, *who lingers at the door*.

SHAWN (*to* PEGEEN): Are you wanting me to stop along with you and keep you from harm!

PEGEEN (*gruffly*): Didn't you say you were fearing Father Reilly?

SHAWN: There'd be no harm staying now, I'm thinking, and himself in it too.

PEGEEN: You wouldn't stay when there was need for you, and let you step off nimble this time when there's none.

SHAWN: Didn't I say it was Father Reilly. . . .

PEGEEN: Go on, then, to Father Reilly (*in a jeering tone*), and let him put you in the holy brotherhoods, and leave that lad to me.

SHAWN: If I meet the Widow Quin . . .

PEGEEN: Go on, I'm saying, and don't be waking this place with your noise. (*She hustles him out and bolts the door.*) That lad would wear the spirits from the saints of peace. (*Bustles about, then takes off her apron and pins it up in the window as a blind,* CHRISTY *watching her timidly. Then she comes to him and speaks with bland good-humour.*) Let you stretch out now by the fire, young fellow. You should be destroyed travelling.

CHRISTY (*shyly again, drawing off his boots*): I'm tired surely, walking wild eleven days, and waking fearful in the night.

He holds up one of his feet, feeling his blisters, and looking at them with compassion.

PEGEEN (*standing beside him, watching him with delight*): You should have had great people in your family, I'm thinking, with the little small feet you have, and you with a kind of quality name, the like of what you'd find on the great powers and potentates of France and Spain.

CHRISTY (*with pride*): We were great, surely, with wide and windy acres of rich Munster land.

PEGEEN: Wasn't I telling you, and you a fine, handsome young fellow with a noble brow?

CHRISTY (*with a flash of delighted surprise*): Is it me?

PEGEEN: Aye. Did you never hear that from the young girls where you come from in the west or south?

CHRISTY (*with venom*): I did not, then. Oh, they're bloody liars in the naked parish where I grew a man.

PEGEEN: If they are itself, you've heard it these days, I'm thinking, and you walking the world telling out your story to young girls or old.

CHRISTY: I've told my story no place till this night, Pegeen
Mike, and it's foolish I was here, maybe, to be talking free;
but you're decent people, I'm thinking, and yourself a
kindly woman, the way I wasn't fearing you at all.

PEGEEN (*filling a sack with straw*): You've said the like of that,
maybe, in every cot and cabin where you've met a young
girl on your way.

CHRISTY (*going over to her, gradually raising his voice*): I've said it
nowhere till this night, I'm telling you; for I've seen none
the like of you the eleven long days I am walking the world,
looking over a low ditch or a high ditch on my north or
south, into stony, scattered fields, or scribes of bog, where
you'd see young, limber girls, and fine, prancing women
making laughter with the men.

PEGEEN: If you weren't destroyed travelling, you'd have as
much talk and streeleen, I'm thinking, as Owen Roe
O'Sullivan or the poets of the Dingle Bay; and I've heard all
times it's the poets are your like – fine, fiery fellows with
great rages when their temper's roused.

CHRISTY (*drawing a little nearer to her*): You've a power of
rings, God bless you, and would there be any offence if I was
asking are you single now?

PEGEEN: What would I want wedding so young?

CHRISTY (*with relief*): We're alike so.

PEGEEN (*she puts sack on settle and beats it up*): I never killed my
father. I'd be afeard to do that, except I was the like of
yourself with blind rages tearing me within, for I'm thinking
you should have had great tussling when the end was come.

CHRISTY (*expanding with delight at the first confidential talk he has
ever had with a woman*): We had not then. It was a hard
woman was come over the hill; and if he was always a
crusty kind, when he'd a hard woman setting him on not the
divil himself or his four fathers could put up with him at all.

PEGEEN (*with curiosity*): And isn't it a great wonder that one
wasn't fearing you?

CHRISTY (*very confidentially*): Up to the day I killed my father, there wasn't a person in Ireland knew the kind I was, and I there drinking, waking, eating, sleeping, a quiet, simple poor fellow with no man giving me heed.

PEGEEN (*getting a quilt out of cupboard and putting it on the sack*): It was the girls were giving you heed, maybe, and I'm thinking it's most conceit you'd have to be gaming with their like.

CHRISTY (*shaking his head, with simplicity*): Not the girls itself, and I won't tell you a lie. There wasn't anyone heeding me in that place saving only the dumb beasts of the field.

He sits down at fire.

PEGEEN (*with disappointment*): And I thinking you should have been living the like of a king of Norway or the eastern world.

She comes and sits beside him after placing bread and mug of milk on the table.

CHRISTY (*laughing piteously*): The like of a king, is it? And I after toiling, moiling, digging, dodging from dawn till dusk; with never a sight of joy or sport saving only when I'd be abroad in the dark night poaching rabbits on hills, for I was a divil to poach, God forgive me (*very naïvely*), and I near got six months for going with a dung-fork and stabbing a fish.

PEGEEN: And it's that you'd call sport, is it, to be abroad in the darkness with yourself alone?

CHRISTY: I did, God help me, and there I'd be as happy as the sunshine of St Martin's Day, watching the light passing the north or the patches of fog, till I'd hear a rabbit starting to screech and I'd go running in the furze. Then, when I'd my full share, I'd come walking down where you'd see the ducks and geese stretched sleeping on the highway of the road, and before I'd pass the dunghill, I'd hear himself snoring out – a loud, lonesome snore he'd be making all times, the while he was sleeping; and he a man'd be raging all times, the while he was waking, like a gaudy officer you'd hear cursing and damning and swearing oaths.

PEGEEN: Providence and Mercy, spare us all!

CHRISTY: It's that you'd say surely if you seen him and he after drinking for weeks, rising up in the red dawn, or before it maybe, and going out into the yard as naked as an ash-tree in the moon of May, and shying clods against the visage of the stars till he'd put the fear of death into the banbhs and the screeching sows.

PEGEEN: I'd be well-nigh afeard of that lad myself, I'm thinking. And there was no one in it but the two of you alone?

CHRISTY: The divil a one, though he'd sons and daughters walking all great states and territories of the world, and not a one of them, to this day, but would say their seven curses on him, and they rousing up to let a cough or sneeze, maybe, in the deadness of the night.

PEGEEN (*nodding her head*): Well, you should have been a queer lot. I never cursed my father the like of that, though I'm twenty and more years of age.

CHRISTY: Then you'd have cursed mine, I'm telling you, and he a man never gave peace to any, saving when he'd get two months or three, or be locked in the asylums for battering peelers or assaulting men (*with depression*), the way it was a bitter life he led me till I did up a Tuesday and halve his skull.

PEGEEN (*putting her hand on his shoulder*): Well, you'll have peace in this place, Christy Mahon, and none to trouble you, and it's near time a fine lad like you should have your good share of the earth.

CHRISTY: It's time surely, and I a seemly fellow with great strength in me and bravery of . . .

Someone knocks.

CHRISTY (*clinging to* PEGEEN): Oh, glory! it's late for knocking, and this last while I'm in terror of the peelers, and the walking dead. (*Knocking again.*)

PEGEEN: Who's there?

VOICE (*outside*): Me.

PEGEEN: Who's me?

VOICE: The Widow Quin.

PEGEEN (*jumping up and giving him the bread and milk*): Go on now with your supper, and let on to be sleepy, for if she found you were such a warrant to talk, she'd be stringing gabble till the dawn of day.

He takes bread and sits shyly with his back to the door.

PEGEEN (*opening door, with temper*): What ails you, or what is it you're wanting at this hour of the night?

WIDOW QUIN (*coming in a step and peering at* CHRISTY): I'm after meeting Shawn Keogh and Father Reilly below, who told me of your curiosity man, and they fearing by this time he was maybe roaring, romping on your hands with drink.

PEGEEN (*pointing to* CHRISTY): Look now is he roaring, and he stretched out drowsy with his supper and his mug of milk. Walk down and tell that to Father Reilly and to Shaneen Keogh.

WIDOW QUIN (*coming forward*): I'll not see them again, for I've their word to lead that lad forward to lodge with me.

PEGEEN (*in blank amazement*): This night is it?

WIDOW QUIN (*going over*): This night. 'It isn't fitting,' says the priesteen, 'to have his likeness lodging with an orphaned girl.' (*To* CHRISTY.) God save you, mister!

CHRISTY (*shyly*): God save you kindly!

WIDOW QUIN (*looking at him with half-amused curiosity*): Well, aren't you a little smiling fellow? It should have been great and bitter torments did rouse your spirits to a deed of blood.

CHRISTY (*doubtfully*): It should, maybe.

WIDOW QUIN: It's more than 'maybe' I'm saying, and it'd soften my heart to see you sitting so simple with your cup and cake, and you fitter to be saying your catechism than slaying your da.

PEGEEN (*at counter, washing glasses*): There's talking when any'd see he's fit to be holding his head high with the won-

ders of the world. Walk on from this, for I'll not have him
tormented, and he destroyed travelling since Tuesday was a
week.

WIDOW QUIN (*peaceably*): We'll be walking surely when his
supper's done, and you'll find we're great company, young
fellow, when it's of the like of you and me you'd hear the
penny poets singing in an August Fair.

CHRISTY (*innocently*): Did you kill your father?

PEGEEN (*contemptuously*): She did not. She hit himself with a
worn pick, and the rusted poison did corrode his blood the
way he never overed it, and died after. That was a sneaky
kind of murder did win small glory with the boys itself. (*She
crosses to* CHRISTY'S *left.*)

WIDOW QUIN (*with good-humour*): If it didn't, maybe all
knows a widow woman has buried her children and destroyed her man is a wiser comrade for a young lad than a
girl, the like of you, who'd go helter-skeltering after any
man would let you a wink upon the road.

PEGEEN (*breaking out into wild rage*): And you'll say that, Widow
Quin, and you gasping with the rage you had racing the
hill beyond to look on his face.

WIDOW QUIN (*laughing derisively*): Me, is it? Well, Father
Reilly has cuteness to divide you now. (*She pulls* CHRISTY
up.) There's great temptation in a man did slay his da, and
we'd best be going, young fellow; so rise up and come with
me.

PEGEEN (*seizing his arm*): He'll not stir. He's pot-boy in this
place, and I'll not have him stolen off and kidnapped while
himself's abroad.

WIDOW QUIN: It'd be a crazy pot-boy'd lodge him in the
shebeen where he works by day, so you'd have a right to
come on, young fellow, till you see my little houseen, a
perch off on the rising hill.

PEGEEN: Wait till morning, Christy Mahon. Wait till you lay
eyes on her leaky thatch is growing more pasture for her

buck goat than her square of fields, and she without a tramp itself to keep in order her place at all.

WIDOW QUIN: When you see me contriving in my little gardens, Christy Mahon, you'll swear the Lord God formed me to be living lone, and that there isn't my match in Mayo for thatching, or mowing, or shearing a sheep.

PEGEEN (*with noisy scorn*): It's true the Lord formed you to contrive indeed. Doesn't the world know you reared a black ram at your own breast, so that the Lord Bishop of Connaught felt the elements of a Christian, and he eating it after in a kidney stew? Doesn't the world know you've been seen shaving the foxy skipper from France for a three-penny bit and a sop of grass tobacco would wring the liver from a mountain goat you'd meet leaping the hills?

WIDOW QUIN (*with amusement*): Do you hear her now, young fellow? Do you hear the way she'll be rating at your own self when a week is by?

PEGEEN (*to* CHRISTY): Don't heed her. Tell her to go on into her pigsty and not plague us here.

WIDOW QUIN: I'm going; but he'll come with me.

PEGEEN (*shaking him*): Are you dumb, young fellow?

CHRISTY (*timidly to* WIDOW QUIN): God increase you; but I'm pot-boy in this place, and it's here I'd liefer stay.

PEGEEN (*triumphantly*): Now you have heard him, and go on from this.

WIDOW QUIN (*looking round the room*): It's lonesome this hour crossing the hill, and if he won't come along with me, I'd have a right maybe to stop this night with yourselves. Let me stretch out on the settle, Pegeen Mike; and himself can lie by the hearth.

PEGEEN (*short and fiercely*): Faith, I won't. Quit off or I will send you now.

WIDOW QUIN (*gathering her shawl up*): Well, it's a terror to be aged a score. (*To* CHRISTY.) God bless you now, young fellow, and let you be wary, or there's right torment will await you here if you go romancing with her like, and she waiting only, as they bade me say, on a sheepskin parchment to be wed with Shawn Keogh of Killakeen.

CHRISTY (*going to* PEGEEN *as she bolts the door*): What's that she's after saying?

PEGEEN: Lies and blather, you've no call to mind. Well, isn't Shawn Keogh an impudent fellow to send up spying on me? Wait till I lay my hands on him. Let him wait, I'm saying.

CHRISTY: And you're not wedding him at all?

PEGEEN: I wouldn't wed him if a bishop came walking for to join us here.

CHRISTY: That God in glory may be thanked for that.

PEGEEN: There's your bed now. I've put a quilt upon you I'm after quilting a while since with my own two hands, and you'd best stretch out now for your sleep, and may God give you a good rest till I call you in the morning when the cocks will crow.

CHRISTY (*as she goes to inner room*): May God and Mary and St Patrick bless you and reward you for your kindly talk. (*She shuts the door behind her. He settles his bed slowly, feeling the quilt with immense satisfaction.*) Well, it's a clean bed and soft with it, and it's great luck and company I've won me in the end of time – two fine women fighting for the likes of me – till I'm thinking this night wasn't I a foolish fellow not to kill my father in the years gone by.

CURTAIN

ACT TWO

Scene as before. Brilliant morning light. CHRISTY, *looking bright and cheerful, is cleaning a girl's boots.*

CHRISTY (*to himself, counting jugs on dresser*): Half a hundred beyond. Ten there. A score that's above. Eighty jugs. Six cups and a broken one. Two plates. A power of glasses. Bottles, a school-master'd be hard set to count, and enough in them, I'm thinking, to drunken all the wealth and wisdom of the County Clare. (*He puts down the boot carefully.*) There's her boots now, nice and decent for her evening use, and isn't it grand brushes she has? (*He puts them down and goes by degrees to the looking-glass.*) Well, this'd be a fine place to be my whole life talking out with swearing Christians, in place of my old dogs and cat; and I stalking around, smoking my pipe and drinking my fill, and never a day's work but drawing a cork an odd time, or wiping a glass, or rinsing out a shiny tumbler for a decent man. (*He takes the looking-glass from the wall and puts it on the back of a chair; then sits down in front of it and begins washing his face.*) Didn't I know rightly I was handsome, though it was the divil's own mirror we had beyond, would twist a squint across an angel's brow; and I'll be growing fine from this day, the way I'll have a soft lovely skin on me and won't be the like of the clumsy young fellows do be ploughing all times in the earth and dung. (*He starts.*) Is she coming again? (*He looks out.*) Stranger girls. God help me, where'll I hide myself away and my long neck naked to the world? (*He looks out.*) I'd best go to the room maybe till I'm dressed again.

He gathers up his coat and the looking-glass, and runs into the inner room. The door is pushed open, and SUSAN BRADY *looks in, and knocks on door.*

SUSAN: There's nobody in it. (*Knocks again.*)

NELLY (*pushing her in and following her, with* HONOR BLAKE *and* SARAH TANSEY): It'd be early for them both to be out walking the hill.

SUSAN: I'm thinking Shawn Keogh was making game of us, and there's no such man in it at all.

HONOR (*pointing to straw and quilt*): Look at that. He's been sleeping there in the night. Well, it'll be a hard case if he's gone off now, the way we'll never set our eyes on a man killed his father, and we after rising early and destroying ourselves running fast on the hill.

NELLY: Are you thinking them's his boots?

SARA (*taking them up*): If they are, there should be his father's track on them. Did you ever read in the papers the way murdered men do bleed and drip?

SUSAN: Is that blood there, Sara Tansey?

SARA (*smelling it*): That's bog water, I'm thinking; but it's his own they are, surely, for I never seen the like of them for whitey mud, and red mud, and turf on them, and the fine sands of the sea. That man's been walking, I'm telling you.

She goes down right, putting on one of his boots.

SUSAN (*going to window*): Maybe he's stolen off to Belmullet with the boots of Michael James, and you'd have a right so to follow after him, Sarah Tansey, and you the one yoked the ass-cart and drove ten miles to set your eyes on the man bit the yellow lady's nostril on the northern shore. (*She looks out.*)

SARA (*running to window, with one boot on*): Don't be talking, and we fooled to-day. (*Putting on the other boot.*) There's a pair do fit me well, and I'll be keeping them for walking to the priest, when you'd be ashamed this place, going up winter and summer with nothing worth while to confess at all.

HONOR (*who has been listening at door*): Whisht! there's some one inside the room. (*She pushes door a chink open.*) It's a man.

SARA *kicks off boots and puts them where they were. They all stand in a line looking through chink.*

SARA: I'll call him. Mister! Mister! (*He puts in his head.*) Is Pegeen within?

CHRISTY (*coming in as meek as a mouse, with the looking-glass held behind his back*): She's above on the cnuceen, seeking the nanny goats, the way she'd have a sup of goats' milk for to colour my tea.

SARA: And asking your pardon, is it you's the man killed his father?

CHRISTY (*sidling toward the nail where the glass was hanging*): I am, God help me!

SARA (*taking the eggs she has brought*): Then my thousand welcomes to you, and I've run up with a brace of duck's eggs for your food to-day. Pegeen's ducks is no use, but these are the real rich sort. Hold out your hand and you'll see it's no lie I'm telling you.

CHRISTY (*coming forward shyly, and holding out his left hand*): They're a great and weighty size.

SUSAN: And I run up with a pat of butter, for it'd be a poor thing to have you eating your spuds dry, and you after running a great way since you did destroy your da.

CHRISTY: Thank you kindly.

HONOR: And I brought you a little cut of cake, for you should have a thin stomach on you, and you that length walking the world.

NELLY: And I brought you a little laying pullet – boiled and all she is – was crushed at the fall of night by the curate's car. Feel the fat of that breast, mister.

CHRISTY: It's bursting, surely.

He feels it with the back of his hand, in which he holds the presents.

E

SARA: Will you pinch it? Is your right hand too sacred for to use at all? (*She slips round behind him.*) It's a glass he has. Well, I never seen to this day a man with a looking-glass to his back. Them that kills their fathers is a vain lot surely.

    GIRLS *giggle.*

CHRISTY (*smiling innocently and piling presents on glass*): I'm very thankful to you all to-day. . . .

WIDOW QUIN (*coming in quickly, at door*): Sara Tansey, Susan Brady, Honor Blake! What in glory has you here at this hour of day?

GIRLS (*giggling*): That's the man killed his father.

WIDOW QUIN (*coming to them*): I know well it's the man; and I'm after putting him down in the sports below for racing, leaping, pitching and the Lord knows what.

SARAH (*exuberantly*): That's right, Widow Quin. I'll bet my dowry that he'll lick the world.

WIDOW QUIN: If you will, you'd have a right to have him fresh and nourished in place of nursing a feast. (*Taking presents.*) Are you fasting or fed, young fellow?

CHRISTY: Fasting, if you please.

WIDOW QUIN (*loudly*): Well, you're the lot. Stir up now and give him his breakfast. (*To* CHRISTY) Come here to me (*she puts him on bench beside her while the girls make tea and get his breakfast*), and let you tell us your story before Pegeen will come, in place of grinning your ears off like the moon of May.

CHRISTY (*beginning to be pleased*): It's a long story; you'd be destroyed listening.

WIDOW QUIN: Don't be letting on to be shy, a fine, gamey, treacherous lad the like of you. Was it in your house beyond you cracked his skull?

CHRISTY (*shy but flattered*): It was not. We were digging spuds in his cold, sloping, stony, divil's patch of a field.

WIDOW QUIN: And you went asking money of him, or making talk of getting a wife would drive him from his farm?

CHRISTY: I did not then; but there I was, digging and digging, and 'You squinting idiot,' says he, 'let you walk down now and tell the priest you'll wed the Widow Casey in a score of days.'

WIDOW QUIN: And what kind was she?

CHRISTY (*with horror*): A walking terror from beyond the hills, and she two score and five years, and two hundred-weights and five pounds in the weighing scales, with a limping leg on her, and a blinded eye, and she a woman of noted misbehaviour with the old and young.

GIRLS (*clustering round him, serving him*): Glory be!

WIDOW QUIN: And what did he want driving you to wed with her?

She takes a bit of the chicken.

CHRISTY (*eating with growing satisfaction*): He was letting on I was wanting a protector from the harshness of the world, and he without a thought the whole while but how he'd have her hut to live in and her gold to drink.

WIDOW QUIN: There's maybe worse than a dry hearth and a widow woman and your glass at night. So you hit him then?

CHRISTY (*getting almost excited*): I did not. 'I won't wed her,' says I, 'when all knows she did suckle me for six weeks when I came into the world, and she a hag this day with a tongue on her has the crows and seabirds scattered, the way they wouldn't cast a shadow on her garden with the dread of her curse.'

WIDOW QUIN (*teasingly*): That one should be right company.

SARA (*eagerly*): Don't mind her, Did you kill him then?

CHRISTY: 'She's too good for the like of you,' says he, 'and go on now or I'll flatten you out like a crawling beast has passed under a dray.' 'You will not if I can help it,' says I. 'Go on', says he, 'or I'll have the divil making garters of your limbs to-night.' 'You will not if I can help it,' says I.

He sits up brandishing his mug.

SARA: You were right surely.

CHRISTY (*impressively*): With that the sun came out between the cloud and the hill, and it shining green in my face. 'God have mercy on your soul,' says he, lifting a scythe. 'Or on your own,' says I, raising the loy.

SUSAN: That's a grand story.

HONOR: He tells it lovely.

CHRISTY(*flattered and confident, waving a bone*): He gave a drive with the scythe, and I gave a lep to the east. Then I turned around with my back to the north, and I hit a blow on the ridge of his skull, laid him stretched out, and he split to the knob of his gullet.

He raises the chicken bone to his Adam's apple.

GIRLS (*together*): Well, you're a marvel! Oh, God bless you! You're the lad, surely!

SUSAN: I'm thinking the Lord God sent him this road to make a second husband to the Widow Quin, and she with a great yearning to be wedded, though all dread her here. Lift him on her knee, Sara Tansey.

WIDOW QUIN: Don't tease him.

SARA (*going over to the dresser and counter very quickly. and getting two glasses and porter*): You're heroes, surely, and let you drink a supeen with your arms linked like the out-landish lovers in the sailor's song. (*She links their arms and gives them the glasses.*) There now. Drink a health to the wonders of the western world, the pirates, preachers, poteen-makers, with the jobbing jockies; parching peelers, and the juries fill their stomachs selling judgments of the English law.

Brandishing the bottle.

WIDOW QUIN: That's a right toast, Sara Tansey. Now, Christy.

They drink with their arms linked, he drinking with his left hand, she with her right. As they are drinking, PEGEEN MIKE comes in with a milk-can and stands aghast. They all spring away from CHRISTY. He goes down left. WIDOW QUIN remains seated.

PEGEEN (*angrily, to SARA*): What is it you're wanting?

SARA (*twisting her apron*): An ounce of tobacco.

PEGEEN: Have you tuppence?

SARA: I've forgotten my purse.

PEGEEN: Then you'd best be getting it and not be fooling us here. (*To the* WIDOW QUIN, *with more elaborate scorn.*) And what is it you're wanting, Widow Quin?

WIDOW QUINN (*insolently*): A penn'orth of starch.

PEGEEN (*breaking out*): And you without a white shift or shirt in your whole family since the drying of the flood. I've no starch for the like of you, and let you walk on now to Killamuck.

WIDOW QUIN (*turning to* CHRISTY, *as she goes out with the girls*): Well, you're mighty huffy this day, Pegeen Mike, and you, young fellow, let you not forget the sports and racing when the noon is by.

They go out.

PEGEEN (*imperiously*): Fling out that rubbish and put them cups away. (CHRISTY *tidies away in great haste.*) Shove in the bench by the wall. (*He does so.*) And hang that glass on the nail. What disturbed it at all?

CHRISTY (*very meekly*): I was making myself decent only, and this a fine country for young lovely girls.

PEGEEN (*sharply*): Whisht your talking of girls.

Goes to counter on right.

CHRISTY: Wouldn't any wish to be decent in a place...

PEGEEN: Whisht, I'm saying.

CHRISTY (*looks at her face for a moment with great misgivings, then as a last effort takes up a loy, and goes towards her, with feigned assurance*): It was with a loy the like of that I killed my father.

PEGEEN (*still sharply*): You've told me that story six times since the dawn of day.

CHRISTY (*reproachfully*): It's a queer thing you wouldn't care to be hearing it and them girls after walking four miles to be listening to me now.

PEGEEN (*turning round astonished*): Four miles!

CHRISTY (*apologetically*): Didn't himself say there were only bona fides living in the place?

PEGEEN: It's bona fides by the road they are, but that lot came over the river lepping the stones. It's not three perches when you go like that, and I was down this morning looking on the papers the post-boy does have in his bag. (*With meaning and emphasis.*) For there was great news this day, Christopher Mahon. (*She goes into room on left.*)

CHRISTY (*suspiciously*): Is it news of my murder?

PEGEEN (*inside*): Murder, indeed!

CHRISTY (*loudly*): A murdered da?

PEGEEN (*coming in again and crossing right*): There was not, but a story filled half a page of the hanging of a man. Ah, that should be a fearful end, young fellow, and it worst of all for a man destroyed his da; for the like of him would get small mercies, and when it's dead he is they'd put him in a narrow grave, with cheap sacking wrapping round him, and pour down quicklime on his head, the way you'd see a woman pouring any frishfrash from a cup.

CHRISTY (*very miserably*): Oh, God help me! Are you thinking I'm safe? You were saying at the fall of night I was shut of jeopardy and I here with yourselves.

PEGEEN (*severely*): You'll be shut of jeopardy no place if you go talking with a pack of wild girls the like of them do be walking abroad with the peelers, talking whispers at the fall of night.

CHRISTY (*with terror*): And you're thinking they'd tell?

PEGEEN (*with mock sympathy*): Who knows, God help you?

CHRISTY (*loudly*): What joy would they have to bring hanging to the likes of me?

PEGEEN: It's queer joys they have, and who knows the thing they'd do, if it'd make the green stones cry itself to think of you swaying and swiggling at the butt of a rope, and you with a fine stout neck, God bless you! the way you'd be a half an hour, in great anguish, getting your death.

CHRISTY (*getting his boots and putting them on*): If there's that terror of them, it'd be best, maybe, I went on wandering like Esau or Cain and Abel on the sides of Neifin or the Erris plain.

PEGEEN (*beginning to play with him*): It would, maybe, for I've heard the Circuit Judges this place is a heartless crew.

CHRISTY (*bitterly*): It's more than Judges this place is a heartless crew. (*Looking up at her.*) And isn't it a poor thing to be starting again, and I a lonesome fellow will be looking out on women and girls the way the needy fallen spirits do be looking on the Lord?

PEGEEN: What call have you to be that lonesome when there's poor girls walking Mayo in their thousands now?

CHRISTY (*grimly*): It's well you know what call I have. It's well you know it's a lonesome thing to be passing small towns with the lights shining sideways when the night is down, or going in strange places with a dog noising before you and a dog noising behind, or drawn to the cities where you'd hear a voice kissing and talking deep love in every shadow of the ditch, and you passing on with an empty, hungry stomach failing from your heart.

PEGEEN: I'm thinking you're an odd man, Christy Mahon. The oddest walking fellow I ever set my eyes on to this hour to-day.

CHRISTY: What would any be but odd men and they living lonesome in the world?

PEGEEN: I'm not odd, and I'm my whole life with my father only.

CHRISTY (*with infinite admiration*): How would a lovely, handsome woman the like of you be lonesome when all men should be thronging around to hear the sweetness of your voice, and the little infant children should be pestering your steps, I'm thinking and you walking the roads.

PEGEEN: I'm hard set to know what way a coaxing fellow the like of yourself should be lonesome either.

CHRISTY: Coaxing?

PEGEEN: Would you have me think a man never talked with the girls would have the words you've spoken to-day? It's only letting on you are to be lonesome, the way you'd get around me now.

CHRISTY: I wish to God I was letting on; but I was lonesome all times, and born lonesome, I'm thinking, as the moon of dawn. (*Going to door.*)

PEGEEN (*puzzled by his talk*): Well, it's a story I'm not understanding at all why you'd be worse than another, Christy Mahon, and you a fine lad with the great savagery to destroy your da.

CHRISTY: It's a little I'm understanding myself, saving only that my heart's scalded this day, and I going off stretching out the earth between us, the way I'll not be waking near you another dawn of the year till the two of us do arise to hope or judgment with the saints of God, and now I'd best be going with my wattle in my hand, for hanging is a poor thing (*turning to go*), and it's little welcome only is left me in this house to-day.

PEGEEN (*sharply*): Christy. (*He turns round.*) Come here to me. (*He goes towards her.*) Lay down that switch and throw some sods on the fire. You're pot-boy in this place, and I'll not have you mitch off from us now.

CHRISTY: You were saying I'd be hanged if I stay.

PEGEEN (*quite kindly at last*): I'm after going down and reading the fearful crimes of Ireland for two weeks or three, and there wasn't a word of your murder. (*Getting up and going over to the counter.*) They've likely not found the body. You're safe so with ourselves.

CHRISTY (*astonished, slowly*): It's making game of me you were (*following her with fearful joy*), and I can stay so, working at your side, and I not lonesome from this mortal day.

PEGEEN: What's to hinder you staying, except the widow woman or the young girls would inveigle you off?

CHRISTY (*with rapture*): And I'll have your words from this day filling my ears, and that look is come upon you meeting my two eyes, and I watching you loafing around in the warm sun, or rinsing your ankles when the night is come.

PEGEEN (*kindly, but a little embarrassed*): I'm thinking you'll be a loyal young lad to have working around, and if you vexed me a while since with your leaguing with the girls, I wouldn't give a thraneen for a lad hadn't a mighty spirit in him and a gamey heart.

   SHAWN KEOGH *runs in carrying a cleeve on his back, followed by the* WIDOW QUIN.

SHAWN (*to* PEGEEN): I was passing below, and I seen your mountainy sheep eating cabbages in Jimmy's field. Run up or they'll be bursting, surely.

PEGEEN: Oh, God mend them!

   She puts a shawl over her head and runs out.

CHRISTY (*looking from one to the other. Still in high spirits*): I'd best go to her aid maybe. I'm handy with ewes.

WIDOW QUIN (*closing the door*): She can do that much, and there is Shaneen has long speeches for to tell you now.

   She sits down with an amused smile.

SHAWN (*taking something from his pocket and offering it to* CHRISTY): Do you see that, mister?

CHRISTY (*looking at it*): The half of a ticket to the Western States!

SHAWN (*trembling with anxiety*): I'll give it to you and my new hat (*pulling it out of hamper*); and my breeches with the double seat (*pulling it out*); and my new coat is woven from the blackest shearings for three miles around (*giving him the coat*); I'll give you the whole of them, and my blessing, and the blessing of Father Reilly itself, maybe, if you'll quit from this and leave us in the peace we had till last night at the fall of dark.

CHRISTY (*with a new arrogance*): And for what is it you're wanting to get shut of me?

SHAWN (*looking to the* WIDOW *for help*): I'm a poor scholar with middling faculties to coin a lie, so I'll tell you the truth, Christy Mahon. I'm wedding with Pegeen beyond, and I don't think well of having a clever, fearless man the like of you dwelling in her house.

CHRISTY (*almost pugnaciously*): And you'd be using bribery for to banish me?

SHAWN (*in an imploring voice*): Let you not take it badly, mister honey; isn't beyond the best place for you, where you'll have golden chains and shiny coats and you riding upon hunters with the ladies of the land.

He makes an eager sign to the WIDOW QUIN *to come to help him.*

WIDOW QUIN (*coming over*): It's true for him, and you'd best quit off and not have that poor girl setting her mind on you, for there's Shaneen thinks she wouldn't suit you, though all is saying that she'll wed you now.

CHRISTY *beams with delight.*

SHAWN (*in terrified earnest*): She wouldn't suit you, and she with the divil's own temper the way you'd be strangling one another in a score of days. (*He makes the movement of strangling with his hands.*) It's the like of me only that she's fit for; a quiet simple fellow wouldn't raise a hand upon her if she scratched itself.

WIDOW QUIN (*putting* SHAWN'S *hat on* CHRISTY): Fit them clothes on you anyhow, young fellow, and he'd maybe loan them to you for the sports. (*Pushing him towards inner door.*) Fit them on and you can give your answer when you have them tried.

CHRISTY (*beaming, delighted with the clothes*): I will then. I'd like herself to see me in them tweeds and hat.

He goes into room and shuts the door.

SHAWN (*in great anxiety*): He'd like herself to see them. He'll not leave us, Widow Quin. He's a score of divils in him the way it's well nigh certain he will wed Pegeen.

WIDOW QUIN (*jeeringly*): It's true all girls are fond of courage and do hate the likes of you.

SHAWN (*walking about in desperation*): Oh, Widow Quin, what'll I be doing now? I'd inform agin him, but he'd burst from Kilmainham and he'd be sure and certain to destroy me. If I wasn't so God-fearing, I'd near have courage to come behind him and run a pike into his side. Oh, it's a hard case to be an orphan and not to have your father that you're used to, and you'd easy kill and make yourself a hero in the sight of all. (*Coming up to her.*) Oh, Widow Quin, will you find me some contrivance when I've promised you a ewe?

WIDOW QUIN: A ewe's a small thing, but what would you give me if I did wed him and did save you so?

SHAWN (*with astonishment*): You?

WIDOW QUIN: Aye. Would you give me the red cow you have and the mountainy ram, and the right of way across your rye path, and a load of dung at Michaelmas, and turbary upon the western hill?

SHAWN (*radiant with hope*): I would, surely, and I'd give you the wedding-ring I have, and the loan of a new suit, the way you'd have him decent on the wedding-day. I'd give you two kids for your dinner, and a gallon of poteen, and I'd call the piper on the long car to your wedding from Crossmolina or from Ballina. I'd give you . . .

WIDOW QUIN: That'll do, so, and let you whisht, for he's coming now again.

CHRISTY *comes in very natty in the new clothes.* WIDOW QUIN *goes to him admiringly.*

WIDOW QUINN: If you seen yourself now, I'm thinking you'd be too proud to speak to us at all, and it'd be a pity surely to have your like sailing from Mayo to the western world.

CHRISTY (*as proud as a peacock*): I'm not going. If this is a poor place itself, I'll make myself contented to be lodging here.

WIDOW QUIN *makes a sign to* SHAWN *to leave them.*

SHAWN: Well, I'm going measuring the racecourse while the tide is low, so I'll leave you the garments and my blessing for the sports to-day. God bless you! (*He wriggles out.*)

WIDOW QUIN (*admiring* CHRISTY): Well, you're mighty spruce, young fellow. Sit down now while you're quiet till you talk with me.

CHRISTY (*swaggering*): I'm going abroad on the hillside for to seek Pegeen.

WIDOW QUIN: You'll have time and plenty for to seek Pegeen, and you heard me saying at the fall of night the two of us should be great company.

CHRISTY: From this out I'll have no want of company when all sorts is bringing me their food and clothing (*he swaggers to the door, tightening his belt*), the way they set their eyes upon a gallant orphan cleft his father with one blow to the breeches belt. (*He opens door, then staggers back.*) Saints of glory! Holy angels from the throne of light!

WIDOW QUIN (*going over*): What ails you?

CHRISTY: It's the walking spirit of my murdered da!

WIDOW QUIN (*looking out*): Is it that tramper?

CHRISTY (*wildly*): Where'll I hide my poor body from that ghost of hell?

The door is pushed open, and old MAHON *appears on threshhold.* CHRISTY *darts in behind door.*

WIDOW QUIN (*in great amusement*): God save you, my poor man.

MAHON (*gruffly*): Did you see a young lad passing this way in the early morning or the fall of night?

WIDOW QUIN: You're a queer kind to walk in not saluting at all.

MAHON: Did you see the young lad?

WIDOW QUIN (*stiffly*): What kind was he?

MAHON: An ugly young streeler with a murderous gob on him, and a little switch in his hand. I met a tramper seen him coming this way at the fall of night.

WIDOW QUIN: There's harvest hundreds do be passing these days for the Sligo boat. For what is it you're wanting him, my poor man?

MAHON: I want to destroy him for breaking the head on me with the clout of a loy. (*He takes off a big hat, and shows his head in a mass of bandages and plaster, with some pride.*) It was he did that, and amn't I a great wonder to think I've traced him ten days with that rent in my crown.

WIDOW QUIN (*taking his head in both hands and examining it with extreme delight*): That was a great blow. And who hit you? A robber maybe?

MAHON: It was my own son hit me, and he the divil a robber, or anything else, but a dirty, stuttering lout.

WIDOW QUIN (*letting go his skull and wiping her hands in her apron*): You'd best be wary of a mortified scalp, I think they call it, lepping around with that wound in the splendour of the sun. It was a bad blow, surely, and you should have vexed him fearful to make him strike that gash in his da.

MAHON: Is it me?

WIDOW QUIN (*amusing herself*): Aye. And isn't it a great shame when the old and hardened do torment the young?

MAHON (*raging*): Torment him is it? And I after holding out with the patience of a martyred saint till there's nothing but destruction on, and I'm driven out in my old age with none to aid me.

WIDOW QUIN (*greatly amused*): It's a sacred wonder the way that wickedness will spoil a man.

MAHON: My wickedness is it? Amn't I after saying it is himself has me destroyed, and he a lier on walls, a talker of folly, a man you'd see stretched the half of the day in the brown ferns with his belly to the sun.

WIDOW QUIN: Not working at all?

MAHON: The divil a work, or if he did itself, you'd see him raising up a haystack like the stalk of a rush, or driving our last cow till he broke her leg at the hip, and when he wasn't at that he'd be fooling over little birds he had – finches and felts – or making mugs at his own self in the bit of glass we had hung on the wall.

WIDOW QUIN (*looking at* CHRISTY): What way was he so foolish? It was running wild after the girls maybe?

MAHON (*with a shout of derision*): Running wild, is it? If he seen a red petticoat coming swinging over the hill, he'd be off to hide in the sticks, and you'd see him shooting out his sheep's eyes between the little twigs and the leaves, and his two ears rising like a hare looking out through a gap. Girls, indeed!

WIDOW QUIN: It was drink maybe?

MAHON: And he a poor fellow would get drunk on the smell of a pint. He'd a queer rotten stomach, I'm telling you, and when I gave him three pulls from my pipe a while since, he was taken with contortions till I had to send him in the ass-cart to the females' nurse.

WIDOW QUIN (*clasping her hands*): Well, I never, till this day, heard tell of a man the like of that!

MAHON: I'd take a mighty oath you didn't, surely, and wasn't he the laughing joke of every female where four baronies meet, the way the girls would stop their weeding if they seen him coming the road to let a roar at him, and call him the looney of Mahon's.

WIDOW QUIN: I'd give the world and all to see the like of him. What kind was he?

MAHON: A small, low fellow.

WIDOW QUIN: And dark?

MAHON: Dark and dirty.

WIDOW QUIN (*considering*): I'm thinking I seen him.

MAHON (*eagerly*): An ugly young blackguard.

WIDOW QUIN: A hideous, fearful villain, and the spit of you.

MAHON: What way is he fled?

WIDOW QUIN: Gone over the hills to catch a coasting steamer to the north or south.

MAHON: Could I pull up on him now?

WIDOW QUIN: If you'll cross the sands below where the tide is out, you'll be in it as soon as himself, for he had to go round ten miles by the top of the bay. (*She points to the door.*) Strike down by the head beyond and then follow on the roadway to the north and east.

   MAHON *goes abruptly.*

WIDOW QUIN (*shouting after him*): Let you give him a good vengeance when you come up with him, but don't put yourself in the power of the law, for it'd be a poor thing to see a judge in his black cap reading out his sentence on a civil warrior the like of you. (*She swings the door to and looks at* CHRISTY, *who is cowering in terror, for a moment, then she bursts into a laugh.*) Well, you're the walking Playboy of the Western World, and that's the poor man you had divided to his breeches belt.

CHRISTY (*looking out; then, to her*): What'll Pegeen say when she hears that story? What'll she be saying to me now?

WIDOW QUIN: She'll knock the head off you, I'm thinking, and drive you from the door. God help her to be taking you for a wonder, and you a little schemer making up a story you destroyed your da.

CHRISTY (*turning to the door, nearly speechless with rage, half to himself*): To be letting on he was dead, and coming back to his life, and following after me like an old weasel tracing a rat, and coming in here laying desolation between my own self and the fine women of Ireland, and he a kind of carcase that you'd fling upon the sea . . .

WIDOW QUIN (*more soberly*): There's talking for a man's one only son.

CHRISTY (*breaking out*): His one son, is it? May I meet him with one tooth and it aching, and one eye to be seeing seven and seventy divils in the twists of the road, and one old timber leg on him to limp into the scalding grave. (*Looking out.*) There he is now crossing the strands, and that the Lord God would send a high wave to wash him from the world.

WIDOW QUIN (*scandalized*): Have you no shame? (*Putting her hand on his shoulder and turning him round.*) What ails you? Near crying, is it?

CHRISTY (*in despair and grief*): Amn't I after seeing the love-light of the star of knowledge shining from her brow, and hearing words would put you thinking on the holy Brigid speaking to the infant saints, and now she'll be turning again, and speaking hard words to me, like an old woman with a spavindy ass she'd have, urging on a hill.

WIDOW QUINN: There's poetry talk for a girl you'd see itching and scratching, and she with a stale stink of poteen on her from selling in the shop.

CHRISTY (*impatiently*): It's her like is fitted to be handling merchandise in the heavens above, and what'll I be doing now, I ask you, and I a kind of wonder was jilted by the heavens when a day was by?

There is a distant noise of girls' voices. WIDOW QUIN *looks from window and comes to him, hurriedly.*

WIDOW QUIN: You'll be doing like myself, I'm thinking, when I did destroy my man, for I'm above many's the day, odd times in great spirits, abroad in the sunshine, darning a stocking or stitching a shift; and odd times again looking out on the schooners, hookers, trawlers is sailing the sea, and I thinking on the gallant hairy fellows are drifting beyond, and myself long years living alone.

CHRISTY (*interested*): You're like me, so.

WIDOW QUIN: I am your like, and it's for that I'm taking a fancy to you, and I with my little houseen above where there'd be myself to tend you, and none to ask were you a murderer or what at all.

CHRISTY: And what would I be doing if I left Pegeen?

WIDOW QUIN: I've nice jobs you could be doing – gathering shells to make a white-wash for our hut within, building up a little goose-house, or stretching a new skin on an old curagh I have; and if my hut is far from all sides, it's there you'll meet the wisest old men, I tell you, at the corner of my wheel, and it's there yourself and me will have great times whispering and hugging . . .

VOICES (*outside, calling far away*): Christy! Christy Mahon! Christy!

CHRISTY: Is it Pegeen Mike?

WIDOW QUIN: It's the young girls, I'm thinking, coming to bring you to the sports below, and what is it you'll have me to tell them now?

CHRISTY: Aid me for to win Pegeen. It's herself only that I'm seeking now.

WIDOW QUIN *gets up and goes to window.*

Aid me for to win her, and I'll be asking God to stretch a hand to you in the hour of death, and lead you short cuts through the Meadows of Ease, and up the floor of Heaven to the Footstool of the Virgin's Son.

WIDOW QUIN: There's praying!

VOICES (*nearer*): Christy! Christy Mahon!

CHRISTY (*with agitation*): They're coming. Will you swear to aid and save me, for the love of Christ?

WIDOW QUIN (*looks at him for a moment*): If I aid you, will you swear to give me a right of way I want, and a mountainy ram, and a load of dung at Michaelmas, the time that you'll be master here?

CHRISTY: I will, by the elements and stars of night.

WIDOW QUIN: Then we'll not say a word of the old fellow, the way Pegeen won't know your story till the end of time.

CHRISTY: And if he chances to return again?

WIDOW QUIN: We'll swear he's a maniac and not your da. I could take an oath I seen him raving on the sands to-day.

GIRLS *run in.*

SUSAN: Come on to the sports below. Pegeen says you're to come.

SARA TANSEY: The lepping's beginning, and we've a jockey's suit to fit upon you for the mule race on the sands below.

F

HONOR: Come on, will you?

CHRISTY: I will then if Pegeen's beyond.

SARA: She's in the boreen making game of Shaneen Keogh.

CHRISTY: Then I'll be going to her now.

He runs out followed by the GIRLS.

WIDOW QUIN: Well, if the worst comes in the end of all, it'll be great game to see there's none to pity him but a widow woman, the like of me, has buried her children and destroyed her man.

She goes out.

CURTAIN

ACT THREE

Scene as before. Later in the day. JIMMY *comes in, slightly drunk.*

JIMMY (*calls*): Pegeen! (*Crosses to inner door.*) Pegeen Mike! (*Comes back again into the room.*) Pegeen! (PHILLY *comes in in the same state. To* PHILLY.) Did you see herself?

PHILLY: I did not; but I sent Shawn Keogh with the ass–cart for to bear him home. (*Trying cupboards which are locked.*) Well, isn't he a nasty man to get into such staggers at a morning wake; and isn't herself the divil's daughter for locking, and she so fussy after that young gaffer, you might take your death with drouth and none to heed you?

JIMMY: It's little wonder she'd be fussy, and he after bringing bankrupt ruin on the roulette man, and the trick-o'-the-loop man, and breaking the nose of the cockshot-man, and winning all in the sports below, racing, lepping, dancing, and the Lord knows what! He's right luck, I'm telling you.

PHILLY: If he has he'll be rightly hobbled yet, and he not able to say ten words without making a brag of the way he killed his father, and the great blow he hit with the loy.

JIMMY: A man can't hang by his own informing, and his father should be rotten by now.

OLD MAHON *passes window slowly.*

PHILLY: Supposing a man's digging spuds in that field with a long spade, and supposing he flings up the two halves of that skull, what'll be said then in the papers and the courts of law?

JIMMY: They'd say it was an old Dane, maybe, was drowned in the flood. (OLD MAHON *comes in and sits down near door listening*.) Did you never hear tell of the skulls they have of the city of Dublin, ranged out like blue jugs in a cabin in Connaught?

PHILLY: And you believe that?

JIMMY (*pugnaciously*): Didn't a lad see them and he after coming from harvesting in the Liverpool boat? 'They have them there,' says he, 'making a show of the great people there was one time walking the world. White skulls and black skulls and yellow skulls, and some with full teeth, and some haven't only but one.'

PHILLY: It was no lie, maybe, for when I was a young lad there was a graveyard beyond the house with the remnants of a man who had thighs as long as your arm. He was a horrid man, I'm telling you, and there was many a fine Sunday I'd put him together for fun, and he with shiny bones, you wouldn't meet the like of these days in the cities of the world.

MAHON (*getting up*): You wouldn't, is it? Lay your eyes on that skull, and tell me where and when there was another the like of it, is splintered only from the blow of a loy.

PHILLY: Glory be to God! And who hit you at all?

MAHON (*triumphantly*): It was my own son hit me. Would you believe that?

JIMMY: Well, there's wonders hidden in the heart of a man!

PHILLY (*suspiciously*): And what way was it done?

MAHON (*wandering about the room*): I'm after walking hundreds and long scores of miles, winning clean beds and the fill of my belly four times in the day, and I doing nothing but telling stories of that naked truth. (*He comes to them a little aggressively*.) Give me a supeen and I'll tell you now.

WIDOW QUIN *comes in and stands aghast behind him. He is facing* JIMMY *and* PHILLY, *who are on the left*.

JIMMY: Ask herself beyond. She's the stuff hidden in her shawl.

WIDOW QUIN (*coming to* MAHON *quickly*): You here, is it? You didn't go far at all?

MAHON: I seen the coasting steamer passing, and I got a drouth upon me and a cramping leg, so I said, 'The divil go along with him,' and turned again. (*Looking under her shawl.*) And let you give me a supeen, for I'm destroyed travelling since Tuesday was a week.

WIDOW QUIN (*getting a glass, in a cajoling tone*): Sit down then by the fire and take your ease for a space. You've a right to be destroyed indeed, with your walking, and fighting, and facing the sun. (*Giving him poteen from a stone jar she has brought in*) There now is a drink for you, and may it be to your happiness and length of life.

MAHON (*taking glass greedily, and sitting down by fire*): God increase you!

WIDOW QUIN (*taking men to the right stealthily*): Do you know what? That man's raving from his wound to-day, for I met him a while since telling a rambling tale of a tinker had him destroyed. Then he heard of Christy's deed, and he up and says it was his son had cracked his skull. Oh, isn't madness a fright, for he'll go killing some one yet, and he thinking it's the man has struck him so?

JIMMY (*entirely convinced*): It's a fright surely. I knew a party was kicked in the head by a red mare, and he went killing horses a great while, till he eat the insides of a clock and died after.

PHILLY (*with suspicion*): Did he see Christy?

WIDOW QUIN: He didn't. (*With a warning gesture.*) Let you not be putting him in mind of him, or you'll be likely summoned if there's murder done. (*Looking round at* MAHON.) Whisht! He's listening. Wait now till you hear me taking him easy and unravelling all. (*She goes to* MAHON.) And what way are you feeling, mister? Are you in contentment now?

MAHON (*slightly emotional from his drink*): I'm poorly only, for it's a hard story the way I'm left to-day, when it was I did tend him from his hour of birth, and he a dunce never reached his second book, the way he'd come from school, many's the day, with his legs lamed under him, and he blackened with his beatings like a tinker's ass. It's a hard story, I'm saying, the way some do have their next and nighest raising up a hand of murder on them, and some is lonesome getting their death with lamentation in the dead of night.

WIDOW QUIN (*not knowing what to say*): To hear you talking so quiet, who'd know you were the same fellow we seen pass to-day?

MAHON: I'm the same surely. The wrack and ruin of three-score years; and it's a terror to live that length, I tell you, and to have your sons going to the dogs against you, and you wore out scolding them, and skelping them, and God knows what.

PHILLY (*to* JIMMY): He's not raving. (*To* WIDOW QUIN.) Will you ask him what kind was his son?

WIDOW QUIN (*to* MAHON, *with a peculiar look*): Was your son that hit you a lad of one year and a score maybe, a great hand at racing and lepping an licking the world?

MAHON (*turning on her with a roar of rage*): Didn't you hear me say he was the fool of men, the way from this out he'll know the orphan's lot, with old and young making game of him, and they swearing, raging, kicking at him like a mangy cur.

A great burst of cheering outside, some way off.

MAHON (*putting his hands to his ears*): What in the name of God do they want roaring below?

WIDOW QUIN (*with the shade of a smile*): They're cheering a young lad, the champion Playboy of the Western World. (*More cheering.*)

MAHON (*going to window*): It'd split my heart to hear them, and I with pulses in my brain-pan for a week gone by. Is it racing they are?

JIMMY (*looking from door*): It is, then. They are mounting him for the mule race will be run upon the sands. That's the play-boy on the winkered mule.

MAHON (*puzzled*): That lad, is it? If you said it was a fool he was, I'd have laid a mighty oath he was the likeness of my wandering son. (*Uneasily, putting his hand to his head.*) Faith, I'm thinking I'll go walking for to view the race.

WIDOW QUIN (*stopping him sharply*): You will not. You'd best take the road to Belmullet, and not be dilly-dallying in this place where there isn't a spot you could sleep.

PHILLY (*coming forward*): Don't mind her. Mount there on the bench and you'll have a view of the whole. They're hurrying before the tide will rise, and it'd be near over if you went down the pathway through the crags below.

MAHON (*mounts on bench*, WIDOW QUIN *beside him*): That's a right view again the edge of the sea. They're coming now from the point. He's leading. Who is he at all?

WIDOW QUIN: He's the champion of the world, I tell you, and there isn't a hap'orth isn't falling lucky to his hands to-day.

PHILLY (*looking out, interested in the race*): Look at that. They're pressing him now.

JIMMY: He'll win it yet.

PHILLY: Take your time, Jimmy Farrell. It's too soon to say.

WIDOW QUIN (*shouting*): Watch him taking the gate. There's riding.

JIMMY (*cheering*): More power to the young lad!

MAHON: He's passing the third.

JIMMY: He'll lick them yet.

WIDOW QUIN: He'd lick them if he was running races with a score itself.

MAHON: Look at the mule he has, kicking the stars.

WIDOW QUIN: There was a lep! (*Catching hold of* MAHON *in her excitement.*) He's fallen! He's mounted again! Faith, he's passing them all!

JIMMY: Look at him skelping her!

PHILLY: And the mountain girls hooshing him on!

JIMMY: It's the last turn! The post's cleared for them now!

MAHON: Look at the narrow place. He'll be into the bogs!

(*With a yell.*) Good rider! He's through it again!

JIMMY: He's neck and neck!

MAHON: Good boy to him! Flames, but he's in!

Great cheering, in which all join.

MAHON (*with hesitation*): What's that? They're raising him up. They're coming this way. (*With a roar of rage and astonishment.*) It's Christy, by the stars of God! I'd know his way of spitting and he astride the moon.

He jumps down and makes a run for the door, but WIDOW QUIN *catches him and pulls him back.*

WIDOW QUIN: Stay quiet, will you? That's not your son. (*To Jimmy.*) Stop him, or you'll get a month for the abetting of manslaughter and be fined as well.

JIMMY: I'll hold him.

MAHON (*struggling*): Let me out! Let me out, the lot of you, till I have my vengeance on his head to-day.

WIDOW QUIN (*shaking him vehemently*): That's not your son. That's a man is going to make a marriage with the daughter of this house, a place with fine trade, with a licence, and with poteen too.

MAHON (*amazed*): That man marrying a decent and moneyed girl! Is it mad yous are? Is it in a crazy-house for females that I'm landed now?

WIDOW QUIN: It's mad yourself is with the blow upon your head. That lad is the wonder of the western world.

MAHON: I seen it's my son.

WIDOW QUIN: You seen that you're mad. (*Cheering outside.*) Do you hear them cheering him in the zig-zags of the road? Aren't you after saying that your son's a fool, and how would they be cheering a true idiot born?

MAHON (*getting distressed*): It's maybe out of reason that that man's himself. (*Cheering again.*) There's none surely will go cheering him. Oh, I'm raving with a madness that would fright the world! (*He sits down with his hand to his head.*) There was one time I seen ten scarlet divils letting on they'd cork my spirit in a gallon can; and one time I seen rats as big as badgers sucking the life-blood from the butt of my lug; but I never till this day confused that dribbling idiot with a likely man. I'm destroyed surely.

WIDOW QUIN: And who'd wonder when it's your brain-pan that is gaping now?

MAHON: Then the blight of the sacred drouth upon myself and him, for I never went mad to this day, and I not three weeks from the Limerick girls drinking myself silly and parlatic from the dusk to dawn. (*To* WIDOW QUIN, *suddenly*.) Is my visage astray?

WIDOW QUIN: It is, then. You're a sniggering maniac, a child could see.

MAHON (*getting up more cheerfully*): Then I'd best be going to the union beyond, and there'll be a welcome before me, I tell you (*with great pride*), and I a terrible and fearful case, the way that there I was one time, screeching in a straightened waistcoat, with seven doctors writing out my saying in a printed book. Would you believe that?

WIDOW QUIN: If you're a wonder itself, you'd best be hasty, for them lads caught a maniac one time and pelted the poor creature till he ran out, raving and foaming, and was drowned in the sea.

MAHON (*with philosophy*): It's true mankind is the divil when your head's astray. Let me out now and I'll slip down the boreen, and not see them so.

WIDOW QUIN (*showing him out*): That's it. Run to the right, and not one will see.

He runs off.

PHILLY (*wisely*): You're at some gaming, Widow Quin; but I'll walk after him and give him his dinner and a time to rest, and I'll see then if he's raving or as sane as you.

WIDOW QUIN (*annoyed*): If you go near that lad, let you be wary of your head, I'm saying. Didn't you hear him telling he was crazed at times?

PHILLY: I heard him telling a power; and I'm thinking we'll have right sport before night will fall.

He goes out.

JIMMY: Well, Philly's a conceited and foolish man. How could that madman have his senses and his brain-pan split? I'll go after them and see him turn on Philly now.

He goes; WIDOW QUIN *hides poteen behind counter. Then hubbub outside.*

VOICES: There you are! Good jumper! Grand lepper! Darlint boy! He's the racer! Bear him on, will you!

CHRISTY *comes in, in jockey's dress, with* PEGEEN MIKE, SARA, *and other girls and men.*

PEGEEN (*to crowd*): Go on now and don't destroy him and he drenching with sweat. Go along, I'm saying, and have your tug-of-warring till he's dried his skin.

CROWD: Here's his prizes! A bagpipes! A fiddle was played by a poet in the years gone by! A flat and three-thorned blackthorn would lick the scholars out of Dublin town!

CHRISTY (*taking prizes from the men*): Thank you kindly, the lot of you. But you'd say it was little only I did this day if you'd seen me a while since striking my one single blow.

TOWN CRIER (*outside ringing a bell*): Take notice, last event of this day! Tug-of-warring on the green below! Come on, the lot of you! Great achievements for all Mayo men!

PEGEEN: Go on and leave him for to rest and dry. Go on, I tell you, for he'll do no more.

She hustles crowd out; WIDOW QUIN *following them.*

MEN (*going*): Come on, then. Good luck for the while!

PEGEEN (*radiantly, wiping his face with her shawl*): Well, you're the lad, and you'll have great times from this out when you could win that wealth of prizes, and you sweating in the heat of noon!

CHRISTY (*looking at her with delight*): I'll have great times if I win the crowning prize I'm seeking now, and that's your promise that you'll wed me in a fortnight, when our banns is called.

PEGEEN (*backing away from him*): You've right daring to go ask me that, when all knows you'll be starting to some girl in your own townland, when your father's rotten in four months, or five.

CHRISTY (*indignantly*): Starting from you, is it? (*He follows her.*) I will not, then, and when the airs is warming, in four months or five, it's then yourself and me should be pacing Neifin in the dews of night, the times sweet smells do be rising, and you'd see a little, shiny new moon, maybe, sinking on the hills.

PEGEEN (*looking at him playfully*): And it's that kind of a poacher's love you'd make, Christy Mahon, on the sides of Neifin, when the night is down?

CHRISTY: It's little you'll think if my love's a poacher's, or an earl's itself, when you'll feel my two hands stretched around you, and I squeezing kisses on your puckered lips, till I'd feel a kind of pity for the Lord God is all ages sitting lonesome in His golden chair.

PEGEEN: That'll be right fun, Christy Mahon, and any girl would walk her heart out before she'd meet a young man was your like for eloquence, or talk at all.

CHRISTY (*encouraged*): Let you wait, to hear me talking, till we're astray in Erris, when Good Friday's by, drinking a sup from a well, and making mighty kisses with our wetted mouths, or gaming in a gap of sunshine, with yourself stretched back unto your necklace, in the flowers of the earth.

PEGEEN (*in a low voice, moved by his tone*): I'd be nice so, is it?

CHRISTY (*with rapture*): If the mitred bishops seen you that time, they'd be the like of the holy prophets, I'm thinking, do be straining the bars of Paradise to lay eyes on the Lady Helen of Troy, and she abroad, pacing back and forward, with a nosegay in her golden shawl.

PEGEEN (*with real tenderness*): And what is it I have, Christy

Mahon, to make me fitting entertainment for the like of you, that has such poet's talking, and such bravery of heart?

CHRISTY (*in a low voice*): Isn't there the light of seven heavens in your heart alone, the way you'll be an angel's lamp to me from this out, and I abroad in the darkness, spearing salmons in the Owen or the Carowmore?

PEGEEN: If I was your wife I'd be along with you those nights, Christy Mahon, the way you'd see I was a great hand at coaxing bailiffs, or coining funny nicknames for the stars of night.

CHRISTY: You, is it? Taking your death in the hailstones, or in the fogs of dawn.

PEGEEN: Yourself and me would shelter easy in a narrow bush (*with a qualm of dread*); but we're only talking, maybe, for this would be a poor, thatched place to hold a fine lad is the like of you.

CHRISTY (*putting his arm round her*): If I wasn't a good Christian, it's on my naked knees I'd be saying my prayers and paters to every jackstraw you have roofing your head, and every stony pebble is paving the laneway to your door.

PEGEEN (*radiantly*): If that's the truth I'll be burning candles from this out to the miracles of God that have brought you from the south to-day, and I with my gowns bought ready, the way that I can wed you, and not wait at all.

CHRISTY: It's miracles, and that's the truth. Me there toiling a long while, and walking a long while, not knowing at all I was drawing all times nearer to this holy day.

PEGEEN: And myself, a girl, was tempted often to go sailing the seas till I'd marry a Jew-man, with ten kegs of gold, and I not knowing at all there was the like of you drawing nearer, like the stars of God.

CHRISTY: And to think I'm long years hearing women talking that talk, to all bloody fools, and this the first time I've heard the like of your voice talking sweetly for my own delight.

PEGEEN: And to think it's me is talking sweetly, Christy

Mahon, and I the fright of seven townlands for my biting tongue. Well the heart's a wonder; and I'm thinking, there won't be our like in Mayo, for gallant lovers, from this hour to-day. (*Drunken singing is heard outside.*) There's my father coming from the wake, and when he's had his sleep we'll tell him, for he's peaceful then.

They separate.

MICHAEL (*singing outside*):

> The jailer and the turnkey
> They quickly ran us down,
> And brought us back as prisoners
> Once more to Cavan town.

He comes in supported by SHAWN.

> There we lay bewailing
> All in a prison bound . . .

He sees CHRISTY. *Goes and shakes him drunkenly by the hand, while* PEGEEN *and* SHAWN *talk on the left.*

MICHAEL (*to* CHRISTY): The blessing of God and the holy angels on your head, young fellow. I hear tell you're after winning all in the sports below; and wasn't it a shame I didn't bear you along with me to Kate Cassidy's wake, a fine, stout lad, the like of you, for you'd never see the match of it for flows of drink, the way when we sunk her bones at noonday in her narrow grave, there were five men, aye, and six men, stretched out retching speechless on the holy stones.

CHRISTY (*uneasily, watching* PEGEEN): Is that the truth?

MICHAEL: It is, then; and aren't you a louty schemer to go burying your poor father unbeknownest when you'd a right to throw him on the crupper of a Kerry mule and drive him westwards, like holy Joseph in the days gone by, the way we could have given him a decent burial, and not have him rotting beyond, and not a Christian drinking a smart drop to the glory of his soul?

CHRISTY (*gruffly*): It's well enough he's lying, for the likes of him.

MICHAEL (*slapping him on the back*): Well, aren't you a hardened slayer? It'll be a poor thing for the household man where you go sniffing for a female wife; and (*pointing to* SHAWN) look beyond at that shy and decent Christian I have chosen for my daughter's hand, and I after getting the gilded dispensation this day for to wed them now.

CHRISTY: And you'll be wedding them this day, is it?

MICHAEL (*drawing himself up*): Aye. Are you thinking, if I'm drunk itself, I'd leave my daughter living single with a little frisky rascal is the like of you?

PEGEEN (*breaking away from* SHAWN): Is it the truth the dispensation's come?

MICHAEL (*triumphantly*): Father Reilly's after reading it in gallous Latin, and 'It's come in the nick of time,' says he; 'so I'll wed them in a hurry, dreading that young gaffer who'd capsize the stars.'

PEGEEN(*fiercely*): He's missed his nick of time, for it's that lad, Christy Mahon, that I'm wedding now.

MICHAEL (*loudly, with horror*): You'd be making him a son to me, and he wet and crusted with his father's blood?

PEGEEN: Aye. Wouldn't it be a bitter thing for a girl to go marrying the like of Shaneen, and he a middling kind of a scarecrow, with no savagery or fine words in him at all?

MICHAEL (*gasping and sinking on a chair*): Oh, aren't you a heathen daughter to go shaking the fat of my heart, and I swamped and drownded with the weight of drink? Would you have them turning on me the way that I'd be roaring to the dawn of day with the wind upon my heart? Have you not a word to aid me, Shaneen? Are you not jealous at all?

SHAWN (*in great misery*): I'd be afeard to be jealous of a man did slay his da?

PEGEEN: Well, it'd be a poor thing to go marrying your like. I'm seeing there's a world of peril for an orphan girl, and isn't it a great blessing I didn't wed you before himself came walking from the west or south?

SHAWN: It's a queer story you'd go picking a dirty tramp up from the highways of the world.

PEGEEN (*playfully*): And you think you're a likely beau to go straying along with, the shiny Sundays of the opening year, when it's sooner on a bullock's liver you'd put a poor girl thinking than on the lily or the rose?

SHAWN: And have you no mind of my weight of passion, and the holy dispensation, and the drift of heifers I'm giving, and the golden ring?

PEGEEN: I'm thinking you're too fine for the like of me, Shawn Keogh of Killakeen, and let you go off till you'd find a radiant lady with droves of bullocks on the plains of Meath, and herself bedizened in the diamond jewelleries of Pharaoh's ma. That'd be your match, Shaneen. So God save you now! (*She retreats behind* CHRISTY.)

SHAWN: Won't you hear me telling you . . . ?

CHRISTY (*with ferocity*): Take yourself from this, young fellow, or I'll maybe add a murder to my deeds to-day.

MICHAEL (*springing up with a shriek*): Murder is it? Is it mad yous are? Would you go making murder in this place, and it piled with poteen for our drink to-night? Go on to the fore-shore if it's fighting you want, where the rising tide will wash all traces from the memory of man.

Pushing SHAWN *towards* CHRISTY.

SHAWN (*shaking himself free, and getting behind* MICHAEL): I'll not fight him, Michael James. I'd liefer live a bachelor, simmering in passions to the end of time, than face a lepping savage the like of him has descended from the Lord knows where. Strike him yourself, Michael James, or you'll lose my drift of heifers and my blue bull from Sneem.

MICHAEL: Is it me to fight him, when it's father-slaying he's bred to now? (*Pushing* SHAWN.) Go on, you fool, and fight him now.

SHAWN (*coming forward a little*): Will I strike him with my hand?

MICHAEL: Take the loy is on your western side.

SHAWN: I'd be afeard of the gallows if I struck with that.

CHRISTY (*taking up the loy*): Then I'll make you face the gallows or quit off from this.

    SHAWN *flies out of the door.*

CHRISTY Well, fine weather be after him (*going to* MICHAEL, *coaxingly*), and I'm thinking you wouldn't wish to have that quaking blackguard in your house at all. Let you give us your blessing and hear her swear her faith to me, for I'm mounted on the spring-tide of the stars of luck, the way it'll be good for any to have me in the house.

PEGEEN (*at the other side of Michael*): Bless us now, for I swear to God I'll wed him, and I'll not renege.

MICHAEL (*standing up in the centre, holding on to both of them*): It's the will of God, I'm thinking, that all should win an easy or a cruel end, and it's the will of God that all should rear up lengthy families for the nurture of the earth. What's a single man, I ask you, eating a bit in one house and drinking a sup in another, and he with no place of his own, like an old braying jackass strayed upon the rocks? (*To* CHRISTY.) It's many would be in dread to bring your like into their house for to end them, maybe, with a sudden end; but I'm a decent man of Ireland, and I'd liefer face the grave untimely and I seeing a score of grandsons growing up little gallant swearers by the name of God, than go peopling my bedside with puny weeds the like of what you'd breed, I'm thinking, out of Shaneen Keogh. (*He joins their hands.*) A daring fellow is the jewel of the world, and man did split his father's middle with a single clout should have the bravery of ten, so may God and Mary and St Patrick bless you, and increase you from this mortal day.

CHRISTY *and* PEGEEN: Amen, O Lord!

    Hubbub outside. OLD MAHON *rushes in, followed by all the crowd and* WIDOW QUIN. *He makes a rush at* CHRISTY, *knocks him down, and begins to beat him.*

PEGEEN (*dragging back his arm*): Stop that, will you? Who are you at all?

MAHON: His father, God forgive me!

PEGEEN (*drawing back*): Is it rose from the dead?

MAHON: Do you think I look so easy quenched with the tap of a loy? (*Beats* CHRISTY *again.*)

PEGEEN (*glaring at* CHRISTY): And it's lies you told, letting on you had him slitted, and you nothing at all.

CHRISTY (*catching* MAHON'S *stick*): He's not my father. He's a raving maniac would scare the world. (*Pointing to* WIDOW QUIN.) Herself knows it is true.

CROWD: You're fooling Pegeen! The Widow Quin seen him this day, and you likely knew! You're a liar!

CHRISTY (*dumbfounded*): It's himself was a liar, lying stretched out with an open head on him, letting on he was dead.

MAHON: Weren't you off racing the hills before I got my breath with the start I had seeing you turn on me at all?

PEGEEN: And to think of the coaxing glory we had given him, and he after doing nothing but hitting a soft blow and chasing northward in a sweat of fear. Quit off from this.

CHRISTY (*piteously*): You've seen my doings this day, and let you save me from the old man; for why would you be in such a scorch of haste to spur me to destruction now?

PEGEEN: It's there your treachery is spurring me, till I'm hard set to think you're the one I'm after lacing in my heart-strings half an hour gone by. (*To* MAHON.) Take him on from this, for I think bad the world should see me raging for a Munster liar, and the fool of men.

MAHON: Rise up now to retribution, and come on with me.

CROWD (*jeeringly*): There's the playboy! There's the lad thought he'd rule the roost in Mayo! Slate him now, mister.

CHRISTY (*getting up in shy terror*): What is it drives you to torment me here, when I'd asked the thunders of the might of God to blast me if I ever did hurt to any saving only that one single blow.

G

MAHON (*loudly*): If you didn't, you're a poor good-for-nothing, and isn't it by the like of you the sins of the whole world are committed?

CHRISTY (*raising his hands*): In the name of the Almighty God. . . .

MAHON: Leave troubling the Lord God. Would you have Him sending down droughts, and fevers, and the old hen and the cholera morbus?

CHRISTY (*to* WIDOW QUIN): Will you come between us and protect me now?

WIDOW QUIN: I've tried a lot, God help me, and my share is done.

CHRISTY (*looking round in desperation*): And I must go back into my torment is it, or run off like a vagabond straying through the unions with the dusts of August making mudstains in the gullet of my throat; or the winds of March blowing on me till I'd take an oath I felt them making whistles of my ribs within?

SARA: Ask Pegeen to aid you. Her like does often change.

CHRISTY: I will not, then, for there's torment in the splendour of her like, and she a girl any moon of midnight would take pride to meet, facing southwards on the heaths of Keel. But what did I want crawling forward to scorch my understanding at her flaming brow?

PEGEEN (*to* MAHON, *vehemently, fearing she will break into tears*): Take him on from this or I'll set the young lads to destroy him here.

MAHON (*going to him, shaking his stick*): Come on now if you wouldn't have the company to see you skelped.

PEGEEN (*half laughing through her tears*): That's it, now the world will see him pandied, and he an ugly liar was playing off the hero, and the fright of men.

CHRISTY (*to* MAHON, *very sharply*): Leave me go!

CROWD: That's it. Now, Christy. If them two set fighting, it will lick the world.

MAHON (*making a grab at* CHRISTY): Come here to me.

CHRISTY (*more threateningly*): Leave me go, I'm saying.

MAHON: I will, maybe, when your legs is limping, and your back is blue.

CROWD: Keep it up, the two of you. I'll back the old one. Now the playboy.

CHRISTY (*in low and intense voice*): Shut your yelling, for if you're after making a mighty man of me this day by the power of a lie, you're setting me now to think if it's a poor thing to be lonesome, it's worse, maybe, go mixing with the fools of earth.

MAHON *makes a movement towards him.*

CHRISTY (*almost shouting*): Keep off . . . lest I do show a blow unto the lot of you would set the guardian angels winking in the clouds above.

He swings round with a sudden rapid movement and picks up a loy.

CROWD (*half frightened, half amused*): He's going mad! Mind yourselves! Run from the idiot!

CHRISTY: If I am an idiot, I'm after hearing my voice this day saying words would raise the top-knot on a poet in a merchant's town. I've won your racing, and your lepping, and . . .

MAHON: Shut your gullet and come on with me.

CHRISTY: I'm going, but I'll stretch you first.

He runs at OLD MAHON *with the loy, chases him out of the door, followed by* CROWD *and* WIDOW QUIN. *There is a great noise outside, then a yell, and dead silence for a moment.* CHRISTY *comes in, half dazed, and goes to the fire.*

WIDOW QUIN (*coming in hurriedly, and going to him*): They're turning again you. Come on, or you'll be hanged, indeed.

CHRISTY: I'm thinking, from this out, Pegeen'll be giving me praises, the same as in the hours gone by.

WIDOW QUIN (*impatiently*): Come by the back-door. I'd think bad to have you stifled on the gallows tree.

CHRISTY (*indignantly*): I will not, then. What good'd be my lifetime if I left Pegeen?

WIDOW QUIN: Come on, and you'll be no worse than you were last night; and you with a double murder this time to be telling to the girls.

CHRISTY: I'll not leave Pegeen Mike.

WIDOW QUIN (*impatiently*): Isn't there the match of her in every parish public, from Binghamstown unto the plain of Meath? Come on, I tell you, and I'll find you finer sweethearts at each waning moon.

CHRISTY: It's Pegeen I'm seeking only, and what'd I care if you brought me a drift of chosen females, standing in their shifts itself, maybe, from this place to the eastern world?

SARA (*runs in, pulling off one of her petticoats*): They're going to hang him. (*Holding out petticoat and shawl*): Fit these upon him, and let him run off to the east.

WIDOW QUIN: He's raving now; but we'll fit them on him, and I'll take him in the ferry to the Achill boat.

CHRISTY (*struggling feebly*). Leave me go, will you? when I'm thinking of my luck to-day, for she will wed me surely, and I a proven hero in the end of all.

They try to fasten petticoat round him.

WIDOW QUIN: Take his left hand, and we'll pull him now. Come on, young fellow.

CHRISTY (*suddenly, starting up*): You'll be taking me from her? You're jealous, is it, of her wedding me? Go on from this.

He snatches up a stool, and threatens them with it.

WIDOW QUIN (*going*): It's in the madhouse they should put him, not in jail, at all. We'll go by the back-door to call the doctor, and we'll save him so.

She goes out, with SARA, through inner room. MEN crowd in the doorway. CHRISTY sits down again by the fire.

MICHAEL (*in a terrified whisper*): Is the old lad killed surely?

PHILLY: I'm after feeling the last gasps quitting his heart.

They peer in at CHRISTY.

MICHAEL (*with a rope*): Look at the way he is. Twist a hangman's knot on it, and slip it over his head, while he's not minding at all.

PHILLY: Let you take it, Shaneen. You're the soberest of all that's here.

SHAWN: Is it me to go near him, and he the wickedest and worst with me? Let you take it, Pegeen Mike.

PEGEEN: Come on, so.

She goes forward with the others, and they drop the double hitch over his head.

CHRISTY: What ails you?

SHAWN (*triumphantly, as they pull the rope tight on his arms*): Come on to the peelers, till they stretch you now.

CHRISTY: Me?

MICHAEL: If we took pity on you the Lord God would, maybe, bring us ruin from the law to-day, so you'd best come easy, for hanging is an easy and a speedy end.

CHRISTY: I'll not stir. (*To* PEGEEN.) And what is it you'll say to me, and I after doing it this time in the face of all?

PEGEEN: I'll say, a strange man is a marvel, with his mighty talk; but what's a squabble in your backyard, and the blow of a loy, have taught me that there's a great gap between a gallous story and a dirty deed. (*To* MEN.) Take him from this, or the lot of us will be likely put on trial for his deed to-day.

CHRISTY (*with horror in his voice*): And it's yourself will send me off, to have a horny-fingered hangman hitching his bloody slip-knots at the butt of my ear.

MEN (*pulling rope*): Come on, will you?

He is pulled down on the floor.

CHRISTY (*twisting his legs round the table*): Cut the rope, Pegeen, and I'll quit the lot of you, and live from this out, like the madmen of Keel, eating muck and green weeds on the faces of the cliffs.

PEGEEN: And leave us to hang, is it, for a saucy liar, the like of you? (*To* MEN.) Take him on, out from this.

SHAWN: Pull a twist on his neck, and squeeze him so.

PHILLY: Twist yourself. Sure he cannot hurt you, if you keep your distance from his teeth alone.

SHAWN: I'm afeard of him. (*To* PEGEEN.) Lift a lighted sod, will you, and scorch his leg.

PEGEEN (*blowing the fire with a bellows*): Leave go now, young fellow, or I'll scorch your shins.

CHRISTY: You're blowing for to torture me. (*His voice rising and growing stronger.*) That's your kind, is it? Then let the lot of you be wary, for, if I've to face the gallows, I'll have a gay march down, I tell you, and shed the blood of some of you before I die.

SHAWN (*in terror*): Keep a good hold, Philly. Be wary, for the love of God. For I'm thinking he would liefest wreak his pains on me.

CHRISTY (*almost gaily*): If I do lay my hands on you, it's the way you'll be at the fall of night, hanging as a scarecrow for the fowls of hell. Ah, you'll have a gallous jaunt, I'm saying, coaching out through Limbo with my father's ghost.

SHAWN (*to* PEGEEN): Make haste, will you? Oh, isn't he a holy terror, and isn't it true for Father Reilly, that all drink's a curse that has the lot of you so shaky and uncertain now?

CHRISTY: If I can wring a neck among you, I'll have a royal judgment looking on the trembling jury in the courts of law. And won't there be crying out in Mayo the day I'm stretched upon the rope, with ladies in their silks and satins snivelling in their lacy kerchiefs, and they rhyming songs and ballads on the terror of my fate?

He squirms round on the floor and bites SHAWN'S *leg.*

SHAWN (*shrieking*): My leg's bit on me. He's the like of a mad dog, I'm thinking, the way that I will surely die.

CHRISTY (*delighted with himself*): You will, then, the way you can shake out hell's flags of welcome for my coming in two weeks or three, for I'm thinking Satan hasn't many have killed their da in Kerry, and in Mayo, too.

OLD MAHON *comes in behind on all-fours and looks on unnoticed.*

MEN (*to* PEGEEN): Bring the sod, will you?

PEGEEN (*coming over*): God help him so! (*Burns his leg.*)

CHRISTY (*kicking and screaming*): Oh, glory be to God!
  He kicks loose from the table, and they all drag him towards the door.

JIMMY (*seeing* OLD MAHON): Will you look what's come in?
  They all drop CHRISTY *and run left.*

CHRISTY (*scrambling on his knees face to face with* OLD MAHON): Are you coming to be killed a third time, or what ails you now?

MAHON: For what is it they have you tied?

CHRISTY: They're taking me to the peelers to have me hanged for slaying you.

MICHAEL (*apologetically*): Is is the will of God that all should guard their little cabins from the treachery of law, and what would my daughter be doing if I was ruined or was hanged itself?

MAHON (*grimly, loosening* CHRISTY) It's little I care if you put a bag on her back, and went picking cockles till the hour of death; but my son and myself will be going our own way, and we'll have great times from this out telling stories of the villainy of Mayo, and the fool is here. (*To* CHRISTY, *who is freed.*) Come on now.

CHRISTY: Go with you, is it? I will then, like a gallant captain with his heathen slave. Go on now and I'll see you from this day stewing my oatmeal and washing my spuds, for I'm master of all fights from now. (*Pushing* MAHON.) Go on, I'm saying.

MAHON: Is it me?

CHRISTY: Not a word out of you. Go on from this.

MAHON (*walking out and looking back at* CHRISTY *over his shoulder*): Glory be to God! (*With a broad smile.*) I am crazy again. (*Goes.*)

CHRISTY: Ten thousand blessings upon all that's here, for you've turned me a likely gaffer in the end of all, the way I'll go romancing through a romping lifetime from this hour to the dawning of the judgment day.

He goes out.

MICHAEL: By the will of God, we'll have peace now for our drinks. Will you draw the porter, Pegeen?

SHAWN (*going up to her*): It's a miracle Father Reilly can wed us in the end of all, and we'll have none to trouble us when his vicious bite is healed.

PEGEEN (*hitting him a box on the ear*): Quit my sight. (*Putting her shawl over her head and breaking out into wild lamentations.*) Oh, my grief, I've lost him surely. I've lost the only Playboy of the Western World.

CURTAIN

GLOSSARY

banbhs (pronounced: *bannuvs*) – young pigs

blackthorn – a stick

bona fide – a genuine traveller, entitled to drinks outside licensed hours

boreen – small track, path

butt – end (*butt of my ear, butt of his tail pocket*)

cleeve – basket

cnuceen – a little hill

curagh – light boat

dispensation – permission to set aside a rule – here the rule against marrying in Lent

drift – a group to be driven, herd (*drift of heifers, drift of chosen females*)

drouth – thirst

drouthy – thirsty

-een – a diminutive, as in *Pegeen, Shaneen, houseen, priesteen* etc.

felts – fieldfares

gallous – worthy of the gallows

hooker –heavy sailing boat for coastal trade

keen – lament for the dead

kelp – fertiliser from seaweed

Kilmainham – a gaol

liefer – rather

loosed kharki cutthroats – demobilised soldiers

loy – narrow, elongated spade for peat-digging

mitch (compare *mike*) – to play truant

pandy – to beat or expose

parlatic – paralytic

paters (paternosters) – prayers

peeler -- policeman

poteen – illicitly distilled whiskey

renege – deny, go back on

Samhain – Gaelic word meaning 'end of summer', a very ancient festival celebrated about November 1st

scribes of bog – patches of boggy country

shebeen – low public house

skelped – thrashed

streeleen – yarn, fanciful talk

streeler – good-for-nothing talker

spavindy – lame with the spavin (disease of the hock)

thraneen – smallest coin

turbary – right to cut turf

union – workhouse, poorhouse

wake – all-night watch beside a corpse

wattle – stick, switch

Western World – sometimes America, sometimes Western Ireland

whisht – be silent

winkered – bleary-eyed

DETAILED QUESTIONS ON THE TEXT

1. How are we prepared in the opening scene of *The Playboy* (a) for Christy's entrance, (b) for Pegeen's attitude to story-telling and lawbreaking, (c) for Pegeen's eventual rejection of Shawn?

2. How is Christy's first story drawn from him? Which details are lies? What virtues are seen in him (a) by the men (b) by Pegeen?

3. What does the first scene with Widow Quin add to our impression of (a) Pegeen (b) Christy?

4. What essential progress has been made in the story by the end of Act I?

5. Show how the scene with the village girls builds up to a climax ready for the entrance of Pegeen.

6. Trace the stages by which Christy recovers from the setback suffered on Pegeen's entrance.

7. What changes in his fortunes occur up to the first appearance of Old Mahon?

8. How does Synge exploit the comic possibilities of Old Mahon's meeting with Widow Quin?

9. What skill does Widow Quin show in the use she makes of the information received from Old Mahon? What are her motives for acting as she does?

10. When Old Mahon comes back, how does Synge contrive to postpone the exposure of Christy until the most effective moment?

11. Christy, with many successes to boast of, is left alone with Pegeen. Notice that in their mutual admiration they are both modestly incredulous of their own worthiness. Show how they echo each other's avowals, even in the formation of sentences.

12. What discordant elements break in on this atmosphere of harmony?

13. How is this conflict finally resolved so as to prepare dramatically for Christy's downfall?

14. After the exposure of Christy, how and why are we kept in suspense about Pegeen's attitude?

15. The last two pages contain a series of new dramatic turns of events. What are they?

16. What is the dramatic value of the young priest in the opening scene of *Riders to the Sea*, up to the entrance of Bartley?

17. What is the importance for future developments of (a) the coffin boards (b) the cake baking at the fire (c) mention of the red mare and the grey pony?

18. How does Synge provide a convincing reason for Maurya to go out while the girls examine the clothes, and at the same time prepare for her return to raise the dramatic level?

19. How is the identifying of the clothes given tension and shape?

20. How does the tone of the play change after Bartley's body is brought in?

GENERAL QUESTIONS

1. '*The Playboy of the Western World*, which escapes definition and categories, is at once realistic and fantastic, bitterly satirical and yet poetic'. Illustrate from the text this estimate by J. B. Priestley.

2. 'A blend of ugly callousness, beauty and joy'. Justify this analysis of *The Playboy*.

3. 'It is the interplay of the dream and the brute fact that that gives *The Playboy* its overwhelming punch' – Louis MacNeice. Illustrate by reference to the text.

4. *The Heart's a Wonder* is the title of a musical version of *The Playboy* recently produced in London. To what extent is it appropriate to the main theme of the play?

5. 'I am your like', says Widow Quin to Christy. In what respects are they alike?

6. In what respects does Christy resemble his father?

7. Who shows the greater clarity of perception in the end, Christy or Pegeen?

8. 'There were five men, aye and six men, stretched out retching speechless on the holy stones'. Find in the play other examples of the juxtaposition of the sorded ('retching') and the exalted ('holy').

9. 'In *Riders to the Sea* the people are simply victims; the acceptance is not whole, but rather a weary resignation'. If this is true, can the play have the dramatic excitement of the spectacle of man *in conflict with* Fate?

10. 'Everything they are doing seems strangely important'. Is this the impression made by the characters in *Riders to the Sea*?

11. What virtues do you find in the primitive life depicted in *Riders to the Sea*? How does Synge avoid sentimentalising the Aran Islanders here?

12. What do we learn in each of the plays about the geography of the immediate neighbourhood of the community?

13. Contrast the evidence shown in the two plays of respect for the dead.

14. Compare and contrast the communities depicted in the two plays.

15. What are the limitations for dramatic purposes of Synge's rhythmical prose?